Fiscal Health for Local Governments

An Introduction to Concepts, Practical Analysis, and Strategies

BETH WALTER HONADLE
Bowling Green State University

JAMES M COSTA
SunTrust Banks

BEVERLY A. CIGLER
Penn State Harrisburg

ELSEVIER
ACADEMIC
PRESS

Amsterdam   Boston   Heidelberg   London   New York   Oxford
Paris   San Diego   San Francisco   Singapore   Sydney   Tokyo

Elsevier Academic Press
525 B Street, Suite 1900, San Diego, California 92101-4495, USA
84 Theobald's Road, London WC1X 8RR, UK

This book is printed on acid-free paper. ∞

Library of Congress Cataloging-in-Publication Data
Application submitted

British Library Cataloguing in Publication Data
A catalogue record for this book is available from the British Library

ISBN: 0-12-354751-2

For all information on all Academic Press publications
visit our website at www.academicpress.com

Printed in the United States of America
03   04   05   06   07   08   9   8   7   6   5   4   3   2   1

Contents

Preface and Acknowledgments

The intended audience for this book is elected and appointed officials and managers in local government; students of public administration and public management, public policy, political science, community development, and public finance; and local government advisors. The breadth of the target audience reflects the complexity of the subject: local governmental fiscal health and condition.

This is an important topic. First, local government is a key sector in the economy. When local governments fail to meet financial obligations, lay off staff, borrow money, or raise taxes, there are implications for the economy as a whole.

Second, local governments are the primary provider of services directly to citizens, both on their own volition and at the direction of other levels of government. We depend on these units to provide services to people. It is hard to imagine what it would be like without local police and fire protection, sanitation, emergency services, roads and bridges, and other services.

Third, what local governments do has a very real impact on the people they serve. Citizens are deeply concerned about crime, traffic, quality education, public health, and the like. If local governments run out of money to pay for services, everyone is affected directly.

But local governments are not islands. Their responsibilities and their ability to finance public services are, to a large extent, shaped by intergovernmental and state-local relations. In the past several years, we have witnessed a massive transfer of responsibilities from higher levels of government to local government to ease burdens on the higher levels of government that are shifting those functions. Local governments have borne the brunt of this devolution, and the potentially adverse impact of these changes on local governments has not received enough attention.

This book has been several years in the making. It has its origins in a program of practical workshops and reports for local governments delivered through the Extension Service of the University of Minnesota in the 1990s. The pilot project was in Swift County, Minnesota, starting in the fall of 1996. This initial project was led by Beth Walter Honadle with the assistance of Mary Lloyd-Jones, who was at that time a graduate student at the Hubert H. Humphrey Institute of Public Affairs, and was done at the request of county commissioners and with the active cooperation of the county treasurer and the county auditor. This pilot project was a valuable learning experience in the political and analytical sides of doing fiscal health analyses for elected local officials. From this prototype sprung the idea of developing a training package that could be delivered to other smaller, mostly rural, local governments.

The Minnesota Extension Service awarded the senior author, Beth Walter Honadle, lead author of Chapters 1, 2, 8, 9, and 10, a generous grant to start the Fiscal Health Education Program (FHEP), which subsidized training and technical assistance to small and medium-sized local governments in Minnesota. James M Costa, lead author of Chapters 6 and 7, worked with Honadle on the development and implementation of this program. They were on a team that taught workshops, analyzed local government fiscal data, and wrote reports for the local governments, who participated in the program for a small fee.

Carole B. Yoho, Associate Professor Emeritus of Applied Economics at the University of Minnesota, was a source of insights into policy issues raised by the seemingly dry numbers that usually told a story if one looked deeper into them. We owe her a debt of gratitude for her work on those early projects back in Minnesota. Brigid (Doherty) Tuck, then a master's degree student in Applied Economics at the University of Minnesota, was also one of the team members on the program known as FHEP and was also a big help in the development of the program in its early stages.

In 1999 Scott Bentley, Senior Editor at Academic Press, wrote to Honadle asking if she had considered converting the contents of the FHEP, which he had just learned about, into a book. He thought the program was targeted to many of the same audiences the publisher's other books and journals reach in the fields of economics and finance. Dr. Bentley thought a book based on FHEP might appeal to upper-division undergraduates through professionals. His inquiry and subsequent support and guidance led to this book, the result of four years of collaboration. The extensive academic and practical background in state and local policy and management of Beverly Cigler (lead author of Chapters 3, 4, and 5) made her a natural coauthor for this book. Her ability to zoom out to the big picture provided balance in a volume focused, in part, on how to make sense of particular pieces of accounting data for individual local governments. Karen Maloney, Senior Acquisitions Editor at Butterworth-Heinemann/Academic Press Business Books, worked with the authors and saw the book through to completion.

We are deeply indebted to colleagues at Bowling Green State University for their help. Robin Weirauch, Assistant Director of the Center for Policy Analysis & Public Service (CPA&PS), and Dr. David M. Stott, Assistant Professor of Accounting, have been team members in the Fiscal Analysis Capacity Training Program, or FACT, which is modeled after and adapted from the FHEP program at Minnesota. Manting Zhang, a graduate assistant at CPA&PS worked on a literature review. Manjula Raghunathan, also a graduate assistant at the Center, was extremely helpful in reviewing literature, editing material, and producing a draft of the manuscript. Yun Li, also a graduate assistant at CPA&PS, helped with revisions on the final draft of this volume. Ten external reviewers provided helpful comments and suggestions on an earlier draft of the manuscript. Their thoughtful criticism and suggestions contributed immensely to the final product. We cannot thank these people by name since the publisher used a blind review process. Pat Sherman, Center secretary, capably assisted in the production of the manuscript.

So many local officials and citizen volunteers have been involved in our local government programs that we cannot possibly thank them all here. But were it not for these dedicated public servants welcoming us into their communities, we would not have had the practical experience on which so much of the material in this book is based. We owe them special thanks for making this book possible and for showing us that such a book is needed.

Foreword

W. Bartley Hildreth[1]

I invite you to embark on a journey toward local government fiscal health by traveling on a well-marked path with three able guides: Beth Honadle, James Costa, and Bev Cigler. This book offers time-tested practical guidance on assessing the fiscal health of local governments in an easy-to-follow manner. It answers the questions of why and how to do it. Each chapter ends with thought-provoking questions designed to reinforce the key points. The authors have succeeded in providing a unique book on an important topic.

This book reflects the special skills of each of the authors. Beth Walter Honadle has wide experience in doing capacity building and informing the rest of us how to make it work. Beverly A. Cigler's extensive set of publications on intergovernmental relations ensures that this book places local fiscal health in a broader

---

[1] Dr. Hildreth is the Regents Distinguished Professor of Public Finance in the finance faculty of the W. Frank Barton School of Business and the public administration faculty of the Hugo Wall School of Urban and Public Affairs, at Wichita State University. Dr. Hildreth was a member of the National Advisory Council on State and Local Budgeting, the Governmental Accounting Standards Advisory Council, former chair of the Association for Budgeting and Financial Management, and a faculty advisor to several standing committees of the Government Finance Officers Association. He is the editor-in-chief of the *Municipal Finance Journal.*

context. Adding additional depth to the book is the financial markets background of James M Costa.

As someone who has served as the chief financial officer of a large city and with over 25 years of experience in the instruction of local government finance, I encourage you to try this book. I say "try" instead of "read" because this book is different from most. Sure, you can read it, but that does not seem to do justice to what these authors offer. Not only does this book have a different style than most instructional texts on local government finance, but also it targets improving the overall fiscal health of local government financial affairs.

I conduct workshops on diagnosing local government fiscal health under a teaser ad that "the Doctor is in." I happily bequeath that sobriquet to this book because the "Doctors are in," and they provide the professional comfort and friendly hand for dealing with that sometime painful, but always useful, course of treatment. Their prescriptions and advice are consistent with best practices.

My goal is to place this book in the context of the changes taking shape in the professionalism of local government finance. Several of the tools deployed in this book emerged from the work of the Government Finance Officers Association (GFOA) and the International City/County Management Association (ICMA).[2] Anyone serious about local government finance must, in my judgment, participate in one or the other of these organizations. These groups continually challenge the prevailing ways of doing things. Springing from their outlets are such tools as the Financial Trend Monitoring System (published by ICMA) and the Ten-Point Test of fiscal health (published by GFOA). More importantly, these association networks provide help in improving management practice and policy, and dealing with the full range of issues and challenges required to preserve a fiscally sound

[2] For information, visit ICMA (*www.icma.org*) and GFOA (*www.gfoa.org*).

local government. Honadle, Costa, and Cigler embrace the fine work of these groups.

In addition, this book helps advance the recommendations of the National Advisory Council on State and Local Budgeting (NACSLB).[3] While obviously focused most directly on budgeting, the NACSLB recommendations encompass the basic concepts of establishing broad goals to guide decision making and using approaches, operational plans, and evaluation methods to achieve those goals.

NACSLB Recommended Budget Practices

Principle I—Establish Broad Goals

Element 1—Assess Community Needs, Priorities, Challenges and Opportunities
Element 2—Identify Opportunities and Challenges for Government Services, Capital Assets, and Management
Element 3—Develop and Disseminate Broad Goals

Principle II—Develop Approaches

Element 4—Adopt Financial Policies
Element 5—Develop Programmatic, Operating, and Capital Policies and Plans
Element 6—Develop Programs and Services That Are Consistent with Policies and Plans
Element 7—Develop Management Strategies

Principle III—Develop Budget

Element 8—Develop a Process for Preparing and Adopting a Budget
Element 9—Develop and Evaluate Financial Options
Element 10—Make Choices Necessary to Adopt a Budget

---

[3] The work product of the NACSLB is provided at this address: *http://www.gfoa.org/services/nacslb/*

Principle IV—Evaluate Performance

Element 11—Monitor, Measure, and Evaluate Performance
Element 12—Make Adjustments as Needed

Source: National Advisory Commission on State and Local Budgeting[1]

Honadle, Costa, and Cigler offer a four-step process for dealing with local government fiscal crises: (1) to predict problems before they occur, (2) to avert problems when they emerge, (3) to mitigate the impact of any problems that persist, and, above all, (4) to prevent any recurrence. More broadly, I see this book as offering four principles for local government fiscal health:

Principle 1—Establish Goals for Fiscal Health, by assessing trends and alternatives

Principle 2—Develop Approaches to Achieve Goals, including fiscal policies, operational plans, and management strategies

Principle 3—Develop a Fiscal Health Assessment Plan, using a variety of tools and techniques

Principle 4—Evaluate Performance, by implementing the Plan and adjusting it as needed

Given the trends and alternatives outlined in this book, it makes sense for local governments to adopt fiscal policy goal statements to guide their actual financial affairs. Fiscal policies state either prescriptions or proscriptions, with an entry based on law (e.g., the city will adopt a balanced budget) or management preference (e.g., the budget will include performance measures). For example, Louden County, Maryland,[4] includes the following justifications for its statement of fiscal policy:

[4] Source: http://www.gfoa.org/services/dfl/samples/BUDGET-Loudon-County-Fiscal-Policy.pdf

This fiscal policy is a statement of the guidelines and goals that will influence and guide the financial management practices of the County. A fiscal policy that is adopted, adhered to, and regularly reviewed is recognized as the cornerstone of sound financial management.

Effective fiscal policy:

- *Contributes significantly to the County's ability to insulate itself from fiscal crisis;*
- *Enhances short-term and long-term financial credit ability by helping to achieve the highest credit and bond ratings possible;*
- *Promotes long-term financial stability by establishing clear and consistent guidelines;*
- *Directs attention to the total financial picture of the County rather than to single issue areas;*
- *Promotes the view of linking long-term financial planning with day to day operations; and*
- *Provides the Board and the citizens a framework for measuring the fiscal impact of government services against established fiscal parameters and guidelines.*

As with many governments that endeavor to establish fiscal policy statements, Louden County adopts policies promoting revenue diversification, budget process, cash investments, debt management, and a myriad of other matters that are important to the fiscal affairs of a local government. Most directly for this book, however, is the formal statement that calls for the application of the assessment tool adopted by this book:

The County will develop, and annually update, a financial trend monitoring system which will examine fiscal trends from the preceding 5 years (trends such as revenues and expenditures per capita and adjusted for inflation, liquidity, operating deficits, etc.). Where possible, trend indicators will be developed and tracked for specific elements of the County's fiscal policy.

Communities interested in a financial analysis similar to what is called for in Louden County's fiscal policy need turn no farther than this book. Not only are the primary tools described, but also several case studies are offered to ground the "theory" with practice. These cases show how to display the data and, more importantly, how to analyze the results, thereby helping the reader fine-tune his or her own analytical skills.

Demonstrating the timeliness of this book, as it was going into final production, the Governmental Accounting Standards Board (GASB) issued a report that defined a government's "economic condition as a composite of its financial health and its ability and willingness to meet its financial obligations and commitments to provide services."[5] Honadle and team directly address these points. Accordingly, this book advances the goals of GASB.

I highly recommend *Fiscal Health for Local Governments: An Introduction to Concepts, Practical Analysis, and Strategies* for use by anyone interested in the fiscal health of local governments. Moreover, I applaud the authors for advancing the work of numerous professional organizations.

I congratulate the authors on creating a new style of book for use both in the classroom and in government offices. This book has the feel of a well-thumbed guide to practice. Practitioners and students should like this user-friendly style. Importantly, it also offers relevant insights on the literature of fiscal capacity, federalism, and public management. For these reasons, the book grounds fiscal capacity analysis in the appropriate theoretical contexts.

Simply stated, this book promotes the professionalism of local government finance.

---

[5] Governmental Accounting Standards Board, "Exposure Draft: Economic Condition Reporting: The Statistical Section," Norwalk, CT: Governmental Accounting Standards Board, August 29, 2003, p. 19.

ONE

Introduction and Overview

[He] may be the savviest public finance officer to date to be burned by interest rates. . . . You wouldn't expect something like this [bankruptcy of 1994] to happen to a county as big and sophisticated as Orange County. If it can happen to them, it can happen to anyone.

Robert Froehlich[1]

The fiscal health of local governments is important. Above all, it is an indication of the ability of local governments to provide adequate, uninterrupted services to their constituents. Thus, fiscal health may not be the ultimate measure of success for local governments. But without a healthy financial condition, the level and quality of public services will suffer. In the words of one noted authority on financial management, "While people want results from government, it takes money to make them happen" (Hildreth, 1997, p. 159).

When the library shuts down, the roads are full of potholes, emergency services are too slow, or there is a lack of safe drinking water, ordinary citizens will perceive a problem. Identifying and dealing with fiscal problems before they get out of hand is better than trying to cope with a full-blown crisis. In this sense,

---

[1] Director of Municipal Research at Van Kampen Merritt, a money management firm in Oak Brook Terrace, Illinois (December 18, 1994, *Chicago Tribune*).

attending to fiscal health is like taking a dose of prevention to avoid the pound of cure.

SCOPE OF THE BOOK AND AUDIENCE

This book is about the fiscal health or condition of local governments. It is based on research and hands-on experience working with small to medium-sized general-purpose local governments in the United States. The book attempts to reach at least three distinct audiences. First and foremost, the book is aimed at practitioners and policy makers at the local level. This audience includes elected and appointed officials and decision makers who are charged with monitoring, understanding, managing, and explaining their governments' financial situation and outlook in terms that are readily understandable by the general public. A second key audience is those students of local government who want to know more about the factors impinging on financial condition and things local officials can do to try to safeguard the fiscal health of their jurisdictions. It is intended to help them understand the context of local government fiscal health and to provide them with tools they can use to analyze the financial condition of local governments. It is also written for professionals who advise and assist smaller local governments in the particular area of their fiscal health. This may include private consultants, state overseers of local financial conditions, and university-based educational service providers.

The primary objective of this book is to help local governments maintain or improve their fiscal health. It attempts to do this by presenting analytical methods that have proven useful for diagnosing and isolating problems. Even those problems that are not amenable to remedy must be considered by local governments when they formulate policy. It will also help local governments plan for a brighter, more stable financial future by giving them strategies for strengthening their fiscal health. And it will help local governments organize, present, and analyze data effectively for both decision making and communicating to key audiences.

Throughout the book it is important to keep in mind that there is as much art as there is science involved in the promotion of local fiscal health and that each local government is unique. This point was not overlooked by a reporter for *The Bond Buyer* who recently wrote about the work of state-appointed overseers of local governments who have gotten into trouble as "the art of saving cities" (Carvlin, 2002). Readers will not find a definitive list of do's and don'ts listed in this book, because what works well in one area might not work at all in another area; or what worked well in one situation might not be politically feasible at another time. States differ in their policies on local self-governance or home rule, so local governments vary considerably in the legal authority they have to make policy decisions; local culture and values determine how acceptable certain actions might be; and competing goals will force local officials to confront trade-offs, leading to different choices from one place to another even though their situations may appear to be similar in many ways. A local government situated on a state border has a different set of choices from a city where local residents have fewer opportunities for shopping or working in another jurisdiction or where some businesses could readily relocate to avoid taxes, for example.

One of our aims was to write a book that will stimulate thinking about fiscal policies and practices at the local level. We are as interested in the unintended and indirect consequences of local government policies on fiscal health as we are in those decisions explicitly meant to affect fiscal health. Changes in local ordinances, outcomes of collective labor negotiations, zoning decisions, economic development efforts, and so forth affect a jurisdiction's fiscal condition just as federal mandates, changes in state financial aid formulas, and the decisions made by overlapping jurisdictions impinge on local fiscal situations.

WHY FISCAL HEALTH MATTERS

Understanding the fiscal condition of individual local governments is important to local officials, taxpayers, investors, and others with a stake in the services and finances of the community. Local officials must be able to understand and effectively communicate their jurisdictions' fiscal situation to people who do not necessarily have a public finance background. Whether they are trying to explain a proposal to raise taxes, cut services, or charge fees for services, it is helpful for local officials to be able to articulate the financial rationale for their actions.

Local government fiscal health is important not only because it has to do with the ability of jurisdictions to finance needed services. There are additional reasons why local leaders should want to improve their jurisdictions' fiscal health. There are compelling reasons for local government officials to strive for better fiscal health, not the least of which is to get reelected by the voters. Other reasons why maintaining fiscal health is important include the fiscal health influences on homeowner location decisions, business location decisions and economic development, local government organizational flexibility and human resource quality, local government competitiveness, service provision quality and variation in services provided, long-term creditworthiness and tax cost of local government on citizens.

Take the fact that homeowners may have a choice of leaving a location when they are or become dissatisfied with the local government. Local government financial condition has an impact on the locational decisions of homeowners who want certain services at the best price available. Lin and Raman (1998, p. 97) find that local government financial condition has an important effect on housing value. Their argument is succinctly summarized as follows:

> *All else being equal, the higher the mix of revenues and expenditures and debt (in relation to the revenue base), the greater the fiscal strain*

on the community, and the weaker the financial condition (i.e., lower the probability that the government will be able to sustain the current level of services at acceptable levels of taxation), with negative implications for housing values.

This suggests that local officials might want to consider the impact of taxation on locational decisions, including housing.

From a national perspective, local government fiscal health is important. As Yilin Hou concluded in a cumulative review of financial management of governments in the United States, "The substantive role of state and local governments in the national economy and in the provision of vital public services requires them to actively maintain fiscal health and stability. The more volatile the market becomes, the more stable and healthy public finance must be" (Hou, 2003, p. 63).

FACTORS AFFECTING LOCAL GOVERNMENT FISCAL HEALTH

Ask a group of local government officials what influences their jurisdictions' fiscal condition. They will likely say that the financial shape their local governments are in depends on a myriad of factors. These range from the weather and natural disasters, the national economy, sectoral policies of the national government, the economic development policies of neighboring jurisdictions, the local tax base, the tax environment in nearby states, the local economic situation, demographic changes, and mandates from higher levels of government, to state and federal aids, labor costs, citizen demand for services, and the discretionary decisions of local officials.

In fact, there are so many disparate factors affecting the fiscal health or condition of local governments that it is a challenge for local officials to sort them out and make sense of them from their perspectives as managers. In this chapter we present conceptual frameworks to help local officials think about how these factors impinge on local government fiscal health and decide which ones are worth their time addressing. Selected examples of the kinds of factors affecting fiscal health with some implications for local finances are presented below. They are intentionally brief and are meant as much as anything to stimulate readers' thinking about actual factors affecting the fiscal health of real jurisdictions.

Snowstorms, drought, flooding, earthquakes, and other emergencies wreak havoc on the finances of the local jurisdictions in which they happen to occur. Depending on their frequency and severity, such episodic events may be hard to predict. Thus, it is easy (especially for smaller local governments) to budget inadequately for exigencies. Because these things are hard to predict, they are often transferred to others via insurance or other means (Reed and Swain, 1997).

Local governments generally benefit from a booming national economy with low unemployment. They need to spend less on social services; tax collections are stable; and property values are maintained or grow during prosperity. In a booming national economy, higher levels of government have the capacity to be more generous to lower levels of government. In an economic downturn, workers are laid off, consumers have fewer dollars to spend, and fewer people are having homes built. These are just a few examples of economic responses that could lead to declining revenues at the local level.

Also, depending on the composition of the local economic base, a change in agricultural or energy policy could have good or bad consequences for local governments' financial condition. A pro-ethanol policy may be lucrative to a corn-producing area, which would be good for the local coffers. Conversely, a program that takes agricultural land out of production affects personal incomes throughout a farming region by lowering the demand for agricultural inputs and for goods and services purchased by farm families. Indirectly, such policies by higher levels of government affect the fiscal health or condition of local governments in major ways.

Some jurisdictions have the advantage of a lucrative and stable tax base. This tends to insulate their local governments from some of the constant problems that beset jurisdictions lacking in the capacity to raise revenues locally through their tax bases. Some communities are fortunate that they can basically send their biggest employer the tab for government costs. But not all local governments have a tax base that includes, say, a power plant or other such facility that has high taxable value and is unlikely to move out of the jurisdiction to escape local taxes. For most jurisdictions, being concerned with developing the tax base is a necessity.

Local governments are vulnerable to competition for local retail sales by neighboring jurisdictions with lower sales tax rates and by Internet sales; and businesses may be drawn to neighboring states offering more business-friendly tax and workers' compensation policies. If a major employer in the area lays off workers or decides to leave town, the local governments that depend on revenues from that business will be scrambling for alternative revenues at the same time that they may experience greater demand for employment, domestic violence prevention, substance abuse treatment, and other social services.

Population changes are another major force affecting local fiscal health. Births, immigration, aging, and other demographic trends affect the demand and ability to pay for services. Following these trends and their implications helps a local government anticipate service demands in the future.

Unfunded mandates for such things as handicapped accessibility and safety requirements, regardless of their merits to society, create costly obligations for local governments without giving them the financial resources to pay for them. State and federal aid programs help fund local services. They create incentives to do things local governments might not do otherwise. But when those funds are withdrawn or shifted to other purposes, local governments are sometimes left holding the bag. This means that they may have to identify and expend local resources on these programs or curtail popular services.

Local government is labor-intensive. A new labor contract with one of a city's bargaining units, a tight labor market forcing local government to pay higher wages to compete for workers, minimum wage increases affecting the competition for qualified workers, and escalating fringe benefit costs, are just a few examples of ways in which labor costs affect local government finances.

Local elected officials attain and remain in office because of the support they receive from the voting public. Citizen demands for all kinds of local services, including education, public safety, transportation, transit, recreation, health, and social services, put pressure on local officials to fund programs. These programs may in turn attract new residents (taxpayers), and the beneficiaries of those services may be willing to pay fees to support them. Conversely, those expenditures may simply drain resources and compromise a local government's fiscal condition.

Local officials make choices about what to finance and how to finance projects and programs through the budget process. Deciding to fund a sports facility by issuing bonds may pay off in the future or it may saddle a community with a major liability for years to come. Investing in expansion of water distribution and wastewater treatment infrastructure may be a wise decision to attract development or it could backfire if the anticipated growth in population fails to materialize. Deciding to finance community development through a sales tax that drives away consumers may be a fiscal mistake, while financing the same expenditures through the property tax may prove to be stable, politically acceptable, and revenue-sufficient.

Reviewing this rather typical and not very exhaustive list of causes potentially affecting local government fiscal health, one thing is clear. Local officials have very little, if any, absolute control over most of the factors affecting the fiscal condition of local government. To have absolute control, the local government would require all of the resources and authority it needed to completely address these problems they confront on a regular basis. In fact, they can do *virtually nothing* about the macroeconomy, immigration at the national level, imports, policies of neighboring state governments, the aging of the population, and the birth rate. As John Mikesell has pointed out,

> *While the federal government enjoys the ultimate financing option of creating money . . . state and local government . . . simply do not have the ultimate backstop of money creation (Mikesell, 1993, p. 19).*

They can do *little* to influence their state's or the federal government's policies on mandates and intergovernmental aids, the market in which they compete for labor, and the demand for local services. They also try to influence the local economic situation to the extent they can by creating a positive climate in which businesses can grow and prosper.

Local officials have *some* control over the means they choose to finance services and about how they invest cash and other managerial decisions. But, by and large, they are at the mercy of numerous factors beyond their control and many dynamics that they can only influence at the margins.

Not only are local governments vulnerable to countless forces beyond their control, but also the home rule powers of cities and counties vary widely from state to state. Local government jurisdictions' authority to raise taxes, set regulations, annex land, and so forth are spelled out in state laws and constitutions. (For the most recent authoritative reference on home rule across the 50 states, see Krane, Rigos, and Hill, 2000). As Gerald Miller points out in the preface to the *Handbook of Debt Management*,

> *The debt management process among municipal issuers substantially relates to law. Tax laws, state constitution, and statutory prescrip-*

tions, as well as local structure preference, dictate what shall be done
to sell municipal securities and, usually, how that sale shall be done
(Miller, 1996, p. v).

THE FISCAL MANAGER'S SITUATION

Figure 1.1 is a slightly modified version of a framework created
by Smith, Lethem, and Thoolen (1980) depicting what Honadle
and Cooper called "the manager's world" (1989, p. 1535). The fiscal
managers envisioned in Figure 1.1 are local elected and appointed
officials who are responsible for the stewardship of the community's finances, and include commissioners, mayors, executives,
clerks, auditors, city managers, treasurers, finance officers, and
kindred positions. The original version of the diagram showed
only control, influence, and appreciation as increasingly large

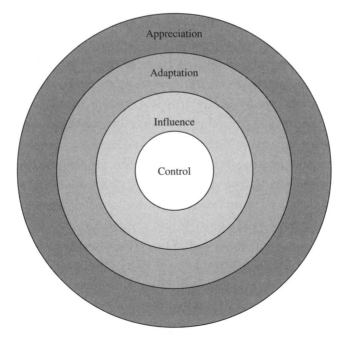

FIGURE 1.1   *Fiscal Manager's Situation*
Source: Created by Honadle, B. W. based on the A-I-C (*appreciate, influence, and*
control) framework developed by Smith, Lethem and Thoolen (1980).

circles in a manager's arena. The point is that managers have a very small area over which they have control, but a larger area of influence, and an even bigger area they must take into account or appreciate.

We have added *adaptation* to the list, because there are important realities to which local fiscal managers may adapt even if they cannot control or influence them. To merely appreciate the existence of these realities may be too passive a stance when there are choices local fiscal managers could make to mitigate or take advantage of them, so we have inserted the option of adaptation. The arena of appreciation includes numerous factors that the local manager should pay attention to just to be aware of them and their potential to influence local finances.

This pictorial model provides a useful way of visualizing the context within which local governments try to attain and maintain their fiscal health. First, it helps decision makers understand clearly that there are many factors over which they have no control. Thus, if their fiscal health is really robust, they cannot take all the credit; if it is really poor, they should not take all the blame. "Policy handles" are merely levers that local officials can use to adjust at the margin the fiscal health of their local governments as opposed to precision tools that can bend and shape the environment to their will.

Second, it gives local government officials a way of explaining the local fiscal condition to their constituents. They can use the model to show that some external forces (e.g., a change in health care benefit mandates, a cut in intergovernmental aid to local governments) are affecting the locality's fiscal condition, forcing the community to adapt to the changing environment with new policies. Thus, if a local government is cutting back on library hours, raising taxes, eliminating garbage collections, increasing park entrance fees, or charging to use the municipal tennis courts, local officials may draw on this conceptual model to explain to their constituents that the jurisdiction is adapting local fiscal decisions to cuts in, say, state aid.

Third, it illustrates that an important objective for local governments is to try to increase the size of the inner circles in the model. That is, local governments should strive to gain more control over their financial condition, in part by exerting more influence over the relevant parts of their environment. By organizing factors affecting local fiscal health into areas amenable to control, influence, adaptation, or appreciation, the challenges of fiscal management become more manageable.

A FISCAL CAPACITY FRAMEWORK

Fundamentally, we are trying to enhance the capacity of local governments to manage their own resources better. Figure 1.2 (a variation on a framework developed in Honadle, 1981) is a diagram depicting what it means conceptually for a public organization to have fiscal management capacity, or the ability to manage their fiscal health better. Within the context of the model we outlined previously, one of the goals is to help local governments anticipate those factors that are likely to affect their fiscal condition so that they can do something proactively about them. Another goal is to help local governments make sound fiscal policies from the perspective of enhanced financial condition. To implement programs, governments must attract, absorb, and manage resources. How well they do this is an indication of their fiscal management capacity. Finally, local governments must step back periodically and evaluate their fiscal condition and apply what they learn from these "checkups" to future activities such as raising taxes, cutting spending, attracting intergovernmental revenues, or other actions.

SUMMARY

From the local government perspective, many things beyond the control of local officials have major effects on local finances. These

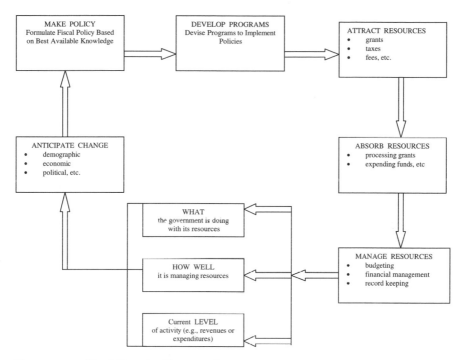

FIGURE 1.2 *Fiscal Capacity Framework*
Source: Adapted from Honadle, B. W. (1981). A capacity-building framework: A
search for concept and purpose. *Public Administration Review, 14*, 575–580.

include policies by higher levels of government, natural phenom-
ena such as weather and disasters, the overall state of the economy,
and economic development policies of neighboring states, among
others. The fiscal manager's prayer might be for the wisdom to
figure out what factors are truly beyond the scope of his or her
influence and control (at least in the short run) versus the things
he or she can do immediately and on an ongoing basis to improve
their fiscal health. In the absence of the ability to control their
fiscal health, local officials tend to focus more on a more short-
term vision just to keep the local government running.

To have the capacity for fiscal health, local decision makers
must have the ability to anticipate or think ahead about what will
affect their finances over time. These influences include every-

thing from demographic and climatic changes to changing demands for local services to changes in intergovernmental fiscal relationships. Local officials create policies that may enhance or hurt fiscal health. These policies may be geared toward economic development and public services that indirectly affect fiscal health or they may be explicitly designed to affect local finances. The programs that are developed and implemented rely on resources that must be absorbed by the government and managed well in order to be effective. In addition, continuous monitoring, improvement, and adjustment of policies will help keep the fiscal health of local governments on track.

In the remaining chapters of the book we synthesize literature, present practical tools for monitoring and evaluating the fiscal health of local governments, and discuss strategies local governments can pursue to help maintain a healthy financial picture. Philosophical issues might make some decisions politically less feasible in some local environments than in others. It would be difficult to say that there is a right way and a wrong way to do things in many cases. Drawing on experience, using good judgment, and applying common sense are often as valuable in fiscal health management as anything. This book is intended to help decision makers focus on the fiscal health of local governments while broadening perspectives and deepening understanding of indicators of fiscal condition and things that affect it.

DISCUSSION QUESTIONS

1. Brainstorm a list of the significant factors affecting local government finances in your city or county. Which of these are things the local government can control? What might local officials do to increase their level of control or influence over factors affecting the fiscal health of local governments?

2. What are some anticipated changes (e.g., influx of immigrants, plant closure, and aging of the population) and how might they affect your local government's fiscal health? What could local officials do to avoid a fiscal crisis or deal with one precipitated by a natural disaster, plant closure, or other emergency?

3. Review a recent change in policy that affected your local government's fiscal health. Were there unintended consequences? If so, could they have been anticipated? How would you approach other policies in the future as a result of this?

References

Carvlin, E. (2002). The art of saving cities: Michigan fiscal overseers face resentment. *The Bond Buyer*, December 18, 2002.

Hildreth, W. B. (1997). Financial Management: The Centrality of the Fiscal in Local Government and Politics, Chapter 8 in J. J. Gargan (ed.), *Handbook of Local Government Administration* (159–190). New York: Marcel Dekker, Inc.

Honadle, B. W. (1981). A capacity-building framework: A search for concept and purpose. *Public Administration Review*, *14*, 575–580.

Honadle, G., and Cooper, L. (1989). Beyond coordination and control: An interorganizational approach to structural adjustment, service delivery, and natural resource management. *World Development*, *17*, 1531–1541.

Hou, Y. (2003). Financial management, Chapter 3 in *Paths to Performance in State & Local Government*. Syracuse, NY: Maxwell School of Citizenship and Public Affairs.

Krane, D., Rigos, P. N., and Hill, M. B., Jr. (2000). *Home Rule in America: A Fifty-State Handbook*. Washington, DC: CQ Press.

Lin, W., and Raman, K. K. (1998). The housing value-relevance of governmental accounting information. *Journal of Accounting and Public Policy*, *17* (2), 91–118.

Mikesell, J. L. (1993). *City Finances, City Futures*. Columbus: Ohio Municipal League.

Miller, G. J. (ed.) (1996). *Handbook of Debt Management*. New York: Marcel Dekker, Inc.

Reed, B. J., and Swain, J. W. (1997). *Public Finance Administration*, 2nd ed. Thousand Oaks, CA: Sage Publications.

Smith, W., Lethem, F., and Thoolen, B. (1980). *The Design of Organizations for Rural Development Projects—A Progress Report*. World Bank Staff Working Paper No. 375, Washington, DC: World Bank.

TWO

Fiscal Health Literature: Drifts and Reflections

Assessing a community's fiscal health is not as straightforward as it might seem.

John D. Landis (1992, p. 501)

This chapter draws on a review of fiscal health writing, which is less like a stream of literature than a confluence. Local government fiscal health is in some sense a focus in search of a subject. It has relationships to economics, public administration and public finance, accounting, planning, and political science. Rather than attempt to present an exhaustive compilation or comprehensive review of the literature on fiscal health, our aim is to distill key points from the literature. Although the focus of the book is on *local* government fiscal health, we draw in some material for this chapter from the literature that deals with other levels of governments as well because of the insights those writings offer for local governments.

What Is Fiscal Health? A Look at the Terminology

This section discusses some of the commonly used terms found in the fiscal health literature. It is important for the reader to understand that there is considerable flux in how these terms are used. Some authors use terms such as fiscal stress and fiscal strain interchangeably. Others make a distinction between fiscal stress or strain, on the one hand, and fiscal crisis on the other hand. Terms such as fiscal health, fiscal condition, and fiscal position are all used, usually with different meanings attached to them. So, with this lack of consensus about the terminology surrounding fiscal health taken as a given, we will try to give an overview of commonly used terms.

Frances Stokes Berry (1994, p. 323) has defined an agency's **fiscal health** in terms of the "extent to which its financial resources exceed its spending obligations." This definition has the virtue of being simple and understandable. What it lacks in detail is compensated for by its clarity and comprehensibility.

Helen Ladd and John Yinger's (1989) definition of fiscal health is "the ability of a city to deliver public services to its residents" denoting a city's underlying or structural ability to deliver public services to its residents, independent of the budgetary decisions made by city officials. These authors distinguish between "actual fiscal health" and "standardized fiscal health." "Standardized" fiscal health is fiscal health without taking into account state assistance, including both aid and the set of fiscal institutions defining service responsibility and tax structure. So-called "actual" fiscal health is the difference between restricted revenue-raising capacity and actual expenditure needed, and it measures a city's capability to deliver public services given its economic and social circumstances, the grants it receives, and the fiscal rules under which it must operate.

A key implication of this distinction is that state aid to local governments acts as a "counterweight" to other trends. (Metaphorically, this distinction is similar to comparing the circumstances of poor people using a measure that looks at a person's income or one that also includes transfers and in-kind contributions that augment a person's ability to consume a standard level of necessities.)

A term closely related to fiscal health is **financial condition**, which Wenshan Lin and K. K. Raman (1998, p. 96) describe as having to do primarily with fiscal effort or the relative level of taxation and spending. They point out "a government could be in good financial *position* (e.g., have good liquidity) but be in poor financial condition." According to these two authors, a weak financial condition means that a government has a relatively low "probability of being able to sustain the current level of services at acceptable levels of taxation (p. 97)."

Fiscal strain, a somewhat general term, has been defined by Terry Clark and Lynn Appleton (1989, p. 47) as a "lack of adaptation by government to a changing environment." Pagano and Moore (1985, p. 23) define **fiscal stress** as "the inability of a government to balance its budget." Badu and Li (1994, p. 9) define **fiscal stress** as "an imbalance between [a] city's revenue-raising capacity and its expenditure need." This term is very much associated with the concept of **tax effort**, which is defined by these two authors (1994, p. 6) as "the portion of tax base that has been tapped as revenue" and "a measure of the effort put forth by [a] government to raise needed revenues (1994, p. 10)." This, in turn, is directly related to the term **own-source revenues**, which refers to revenues that are at the discretion of the local government and thus do not include intergovernmental transfers. J. Edwin Benton (1986, p. 27) uses the term **revenue burdens** "to connote the fiscal sacrifice or effort made by citizens when government collects revenue from them." By extension, **revenue-raising capacity** (Badu and Li, 1994, p. 9) is "the amount of money a city could raise (per capita) at a given tax burden on its residents." Even more generally, Freda Johnson and Diana Roswick (1991, p. 177) define **fiscal capacity** as "the ability of a jurisdiction to generate taxes and other revenues from its own sources."

Whether a given situation is deemed **fiscal stress** or **fiscal crisis** may have more to do with the eye of the beholder than with a rigorous definition of the concepts. As Alan K. Campbell wrote more than 30 years ago, "Definition [of urban crises] is difficult because the impact of the crisis varies from person to person and group to group" (Campbell, 1970, p. r).

The difficulty of defining a fiscal crisis based on different people's perceptions is illustrated by the following passage from R. G. Downing's (1991, p. 323) article on urban county fiscal stress and the perceptions of public officials:

> *Situations perceived by respondents to have the highest validity as indicators of fiscal stress are (1) inability to meet payrolls when due and (2) default on repayment of bonded debt. Since these indicators obviously signify extreme conditions avoided by almost all counties, even by those in the poorest financial condition, they might more appropriately be considered signs of fiscal crisis, not fiscal stress.*

Various authors have attempted to distinguish between run-of-the-mill budget problems and fiscal crises. A fiscal crisis, according to Werner Hirsch and Anthony Rufolo (1990), is "when a government reaches a state such that the normal budgetary flexibility no longer exists. If no combination of acceptable expenditure cuts, revenue increases, and borrowing exists, then the government is in a crisis situation."

Of course, Hirsch and Rufolo's definition begs the question of what constitutes "acceptable" to the voters. As Sheila Tschinkel and Larry Wall (1994, p. 1) observed, "All levels of government have problems funding the programs their constituents want at the tax levels their constituents are willing to accept." This last point illustrates that there are political dimensions as well as administrative and economic dimensions to the concept of fiscal health.

Reschovksy (1997, p. 447) noted that whether a city goes bankrupt is not necessarily a good indicator of its fiscal health. He argues for defining fiscal condition as a gap between expenditure need and revenue-raising capacity rather than just looking at the short-term budget situation.

Referring to Ladd and Yinger's work, Harold Wolman (1992, p. 473) wrote, "Fiscal stress presumably would consist of either poor fiscal health relative to other cities or a deterioration of a city's fiscal health over time." This suggests that fiscal health is a relative concept. Measurement is comparing one unit to another or to itself over time.

Quite recently a team of researchers at Michigan State University developed a new set of indicators to predict fiscal distress with absolute standards. Their indicators are population growth over two years, real taxable value growth over two years, large decrease in real taxable value over two years, general fund expenditures as a percentage of taxable value, general fund operating deficit, prior general fund operating deficits for two previous years, general fund balance as a percentage of general fund revenues, current or previous year deficit in major fund, and general long-term debt as a percentage of taxable value (Kleine, Kloha, and Weissert).

One of the primary stated goals of this alternative approach is to relieve dependence on relative comparisons, a central analytical tenet of the Ten-Point Test. The authors instead propose a statistical benchmarking framework for five of their nine indicators of fiscal distress, whereby the local government is penalized for every indicator falling outside the bounds of an established benchmark. While the objective is sound, the technique has a couple of drawbacks. First, the approach is still fundamentally a relative analysis because it compares the local government to the established benchmark, as in the Ten-Point-Test. Consequently, the assessment of fiscal condition for each indicator is only as good as the strength of the local governments upon which the benchmark was derived. Second, the statistical technique employed, the benchmark being equivalent to one standard deviation away from the sample mean, is subject to the perversions of nonnormal distributions in the benchmarking sample. That is, a handful of outliers in an otherwise tight distribution can skew the distribution and hence distort the mean and standard deviation statistics. The ultimate effect is to compute a benchmark that is too conservative whereby a fiscal indicator that is inherently weak may sneak under the radar of a flawed benchmark.

The four remaining indicators among the proposed nine provide logical trend analyses of change in population growth, repeated negative fund balances, and declining tax revenues.

Finally, the U.S. Advisory Commission on Intergovernmental Relations adopted the following working definition of **financial emergency** for purposes of its 1973 report on the intergovernmental dimension of city financial emergencies: "situations in which a city reaches the point at which it can no longer perform its existing levels of services because of inability to meet payrolls, pay current bills, pay amounts due other government agencies, or pay debt service on bonds or maturing short-term notes because it lacks either cash or appropriations authority" (Advisory Commission on Intergovernmental Relations, 1973, p. 3).

In summary, fiscal health terminology is anything but precise and neat. But there are common themes. The definition one uses may vary with the purpose to which it will be applied.

INFLUENCES ON FISCAL HEALTH REVISITED

One of the key points of Chapter 1 was that local governments are extremely vulnerable to external forces. Here we draw on references from the literature that document some of those forces and influences.

There is considerable support in the literature (Benton, 1986, p. 21; Bahl, 1984, p. 85) for the proposition that the single most important factor affecting state and local government fiscal health is the performance of the national economy. The rate of economic growth, inflation, recession, and so forth impact state and local government budgets and therefore their fiscal health.

In the early 1990s Philip Dearborn (1994) examined the fiscal outlook for the state and local government sector from a federal perspective. He studied four factors: the federal budget, health care reform (including Medicaid), welfare reform, and federal mandates and regulations. He concluded that because of a severely constrained federal budget, state and local governments could not depend on federal funding to help reduce the pressure on state and local governments. He found that mandates, while they remain a potential financial concern of local governments, may not be as detrimental to state and local fiscal health as some observers have predicted.

Steven Gold (1992) studied the extent to which the federal government's policies contributed to fiscal stress of state governments in the early 1990s. He found that they had affected fiscal stress less through reductions in federal aid than through tax policy, unfunded mandates, and the federal government's failure to cope with major national problems such as health care and poverty. He also noted that federal court rulings (as well as state court decisions) have caused budget problems for states.

Helen Ladd (1991) found that the financial condition of states appears to influence the amount of state aid to local governments. Ladd (1991, p. 491) also found that "only when aid is in the form of shared taxes rather than annual appropriations do local governments share fully in the growth of the state economy." Her conclusion is that local governments should be cautious about becoming too dependent on state governments for their revenue. Mildred Warner's (1999) study of the experience of eight counties in one region of the country also documented the implications of devolution for local government finances. She found that "because macroeconomic forces favor some locations over others, local abilities to raise revenue is unevenly distributed across the nation." States, therefore, have a very important role to play in the redistribution of resources to local governments whose "ability to raise revenue is limited in large part by local well-being." Both Ladd's work and Warner's work illustrate the point made in Chapter 1 that factors such as state funding are outside the control of individual local governments.

Changing demographics, another factor largely beyond the influence or control of local governments, also influence fiscal health. William Fox and Patrick Sullivan (1978) examined the fiscal impacts of changes in population for rural areas. They found that total population alone is not sufficient to describe the pressure on local government budgets. However, they concluded that changing socioeconomic composition might have significant effects on the demand for local government services. In other words, an influx of population with higher needs for local government services will not have the same impact on local fiscal health as a different composition of population growth.

Despite the external influences on local government fiscal health, local governments are not without the ability to strengthen and improve their fiscal health. Through the use of sound analytical techniques, good management and forward-looking policies, they can help themselves.

Whether it is the national economy, federal mandates, or state aid to local governments, it is clear that the model of the fiscal manager's situation depicted in Chapter 1 of this book is reflected in the literature on fiscal health. So much of what affects local fiscal health and condition is beyond their control or even influence.

Measuring Fiscal Health

In their book, *The Financial Analysis of Governments*, Berne and Schramm wrote, "the judgment factor will never be replaced entirely by cookbook formulas" (p. 93). Financial analysis, or evaluation of the financial health or condition of governments, according to these authors, requires one to "clarify the goals of the analysis, determine the level [of analysis], construct a framework or 'model' to organize the analysis, develop comparative methods that provide benchmarks . . . , and identify and secure the information needed to carry out the analysis" (p. 7).

In the second edition of *Public Finance Administration* Reed and Swain wrote, "assessing financial conditions refers to evaluating information related to finances for the sake of making decisions" (p. 316). They distinguished between the perspectives of people external to the organization being studied from those of persons in decision making within the organization because assessments are made from differing points of view for different needs (p. 317).

Freda Johnson and Diana Roswick (1991, p. 197) have noted, "The evaluation of a community's fiscal capacity entails a series of analytic judgments based on qualitative as well as quantitative factors." The literature offers a number of ways to measure a jurisdiction's fiscal health. These indicators are ways of taking a local government's vital signs for purposes of diagnosing problems, documenting current conditions, and tracking trends for early warning of potential areas of concern.

The measures typically capture one or more aspects of a local government's financial picture: revenues, expenditures, operating position, and debt structure. For revenues, analysts include all types of income such as tax revenue, fees and charges, and intergovernmental aid. Expenditures typically include everything from debt service to general expenditures and capital projects. Operating position indicators include such things as total cash and investments in the general fund and have to do with how able a jurisdiction is to meet its short-term obligations such as its payroll, bills, and other current expenditures. Debt structure is focused on the long term and tends to include measures like the jurisdiction's general obligation debt to be repaid from property tax revenues per capita. Figure 2.1[1] graphically depicts the

[1] This figure was developed as a teaching tool by Dr. David M. Stott, Assistant Professor in the Department of Accounting and Management Information Systems at Bowling Green State University for the Center for Policy Analysis & Public Service's FACT (Fiscal Analysis Capacity Training) workshops for local governments in northwestern Ohio.

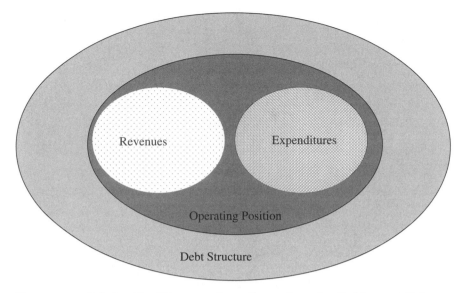

FIGURE 2.1   *Relationship of Revenues, Expenditures, Operating Position, and Debt Structure*
Source: Dr. David M. Stott, Bowling Green State University

relationship between revenues, expenditures, operating position, and debt structure.

It is difficult to argue that one particular indicator is the best sign of fiscal health or that one set of indicators is the best without knowing the intended purpose, the target audience, and the practical constraints on the analyst. For example, if the audience is the general public or taxpayers in a jurisdiction, simple, lucid measures are preferable. If the intent of the analysis is to help elected officials make policy decisions about revenues, expenditures, how to finance projects, and the like, then more detailed and complex analyses will be more appropriate. If the purpose is to help the city manager track the city's fiscal health over time, then she or he may need to examine a host of indicators zeroing in on specific aspects of the jurisdiction's finances. Bond rating agencies look at a wide range of factors including local management capability, overlapping debt, and local economic trends to gauge the creditworthiness of debt for investors. A recent Moody's Investors Service report (Rattner, 2003) said that financial analysis needs to look not only at the past and current conditions, but also at the future with consideration of the fiscal strategies communities use. In any case, the analyst will be constrained by such things as time, cost, technical expertise (Sokolow and Honadle, 1984), and data availability (Honadle and Lloyd-Jones, 1998). If a local government wants to use some of the more sophisticated techniques for analyzing financial data, it may need to start collecting certain data.

Bateman (1990, p. 42) describes the Overall-Ranking Percentiles System (ORAP) to monitor the creditworthiness of individual municipal securities. The system examines and ranks credit according to credit strength using microcomputers. Other experts (Hoang, 1990; Ciccarone, 1990) on local governments also stress the importance of using computers to analyze local government data. Clark and Chan (1990, p. 55) discuss the need to develop an information system to monitor the financial condition and performance of municipal bonds.

Knowing about the various analytical tools, their purposes, their data requirements, their limitations and their capabilities will help guide the analyst to the indicators that will best meet particular information needs.

In Chapter 5, we focus on three specific tools to illustrate a range of possible tools, including a test (Brown, 1993) comprised of 10 easy-to-compute ratios that yields a snapshot of a government's fiscal health, a more finely tuned set of 36 indicators (Groves and Valente, 1994) that is useful for answering particular questions of possible interest to decision makers, and a budgetary tool (Alter, McLaughlin and Melniker) for analyzing budget trends that is helpful for projecting budgets. Suffice it to say here that different tools are available for different purposes and are compatible with different levels of technical skill, data availability, computer access, and time constraints.

Timothy Mercer and Mark Gilbert (1996), writing about Nova Scotia's attempt to develop a financial condition index for local governments, expressed the struggle for striking a balance between comprehensiveness and simplicity. They found that the Ten-Point Test of financial condition was the most practical model, but that

> *Its emphasis on simplicity of use contradicted Nova Scotia's goal of establishing a comprehensive index. Conversely, an index rating for local governments, developed by the Harvard Institute for International Affairs and Indonesia's Department Keuangan, appeared to be extremely cumbersome and reliant upon a great deal of qualitative information. Somewhere between these two models it was hoped that an index could be developed which would include as many measures of financial condition as possible while at the same time avoiding excessive complexity (p. 36).*

Using factor analysis, these authors studied the indicators in the index in which a municipality could receive a maximum score of 100 points. They found that, by and large, municipalities who scored high on the index were experiencing good financial health. For them, the accuracy of the more complicated index was more important than ease of use.

The Governmental Accounting Standards Board (through GASB 34) is now requiring state and local governments to report the value of their investments at "fair value" (the amount at which an investment could be exchanged in a current, unforced sale between willing parties) as opposed to the traditional cost-based (cost of acquisition) standard. According to Randy Finden (1996), fair value is "a more accurate barometer of financial health." He says,

> *Fair value reporting provides financial statement users with better information to assess accountability, the level of services a government can provide and the government's financial condition (p. 8).*

John D. Landis (1992, p. 501) finds that, "per capita assessed valuation remains a reasonably useful gauge of community fiscal health." "All else being equal," he writes,

> *A decrease in per capita assessed valuation indicates that the demand for city services and infrastructure, as manifest through population growth, is increasing faster than the taxable property base. Communities in which per capita assessed valuation is declining need to look for other, nontax revenue sources.*

Hembree, Shelton, and Tyer (2000) recommend benchmarking to help local officials set their individual local government's policies on fund balances. They suggest that studying the prevailing practices of other jurisdictions with respect to fund balances is a good way for local governments to begin developing their own policies. A positive difference between current assets and current liabilities is an indication of the resources a local government has immediately available to finance ongoing operations. Hembree, Shelton, and Tyer (2000, p. 17) lament that "Searching in the public finance literature for help when a jurisdiction wants to establish a policy on reserve fund balances can be confusing because, often, no distinction is made between contingency funds and reserve funds." Their view is that as long as a community meets its basic liquidity needs, the target range for the fund balance is of less importance than that the community has a policy that it revisits from time to time.

Lance Wolff and Jesse Hughes (1998) have addressed the need for a standardized tool for public managers to use to cope in a time of fiscal stress and scarce resources by offering a statement of financial condition for local governments. With this audience in mind, they (Wolff & Hughes, 1998, p. 29) wrote:

> *. . . [P]ublic financial managers need to know their current status before responding to internal and/or external environmental forces. A statement of financial condition must be specially tailored to meet*

*the needs of its users and accomplish its objectives of accountability.
. . . Simplicity and usefulness should be the guiding light even
though local governments are complex and diverse organizations
that demand care and expertise.*

Their model defines net available assets as the liquidated value
of expendable, available, and appropriable resources. They use
this concept to measure and report financial condition through a
tool for assessing past, current, and future financial performance.

Shelton and Albee (2000), in their case study of Myrtle Beach,
South Carolina, advocate for involving citizens (the customers or
stakeholders for local government) in fiscal planning. In measuring financial performance they measured progress on financial
plan goals by using benchmark comparisons with 10 cities of
similar size and type of operations in the region. Their goals
included such considerations as revenue mix, a balanced budget
and competitive tax and rate structures, the avoidance of interim
borrowing to maintain fund balances, and adequate sources of
capital and low-cost borrowing. Shelton and Albee (2000, p. 88)
maintain that local governments will satisfy their customers more
if the customers are involved in strategic planning so they will
know what the financial constraints are:

> *By involving its customers more thoroughly in the policy process, the
> government elevates the importance of their customers' understand-
> ing the financial possibilities and boundaries.*

Once again, the audience is a key consideration in the choice
of measures one uses to examine the fiscal condition, performance, health, and the like of local governments.

Roy Bahl and William Duncombe (1991, p. 194) capture the
measurement problem this way:

> *One of the most heavily investigated and controversial areas in
> public finance is state and local government fiscal health. What does*

it mean and how do we measure it? [T]he federal government may carry out a fiscal distress analysis to determine whether New York should receive a greater share of federal aid, but state officials may think of measuring distress in terms of budget balance or in terms of whether a proposed capital improvements program will be carried out.

Bahl and Duncombe (1991, p. 194) considered three types of fiscal health measures in their study of the fiscal health of state and local government in New York State:

1. Surplus/deficit measures;

2. Bond ratings and debt ratios;

3. Measures of underlying fiscal capacity and expenditure need.

Bahl and Duncombe noted that the surplus/deficit measures are a direct concern to state and local government officials; bond ratings and debt ratios are primarily of interest to lenders and investors; and the measures of underlying fiscal capacity and expenditure need are attempts to abstract for real decisions of the governments being studied.

What Governments Do About Fiscal Problems

When local governments perceive that they have fiscal problems, they respond differently depending on the perceived problem (e.g., high indebtedness and/or low levels of short-term cash liquidity) and the options they have available to them (or know about) to remedy the situation. Several studies have documented the types of activities local governments engage in to deal with fiscal problems. We discuss a few of those studies here.

Some of the actions state and local governments have taken (Benton, 1986) is increased taxes, raised user charges, run deficits or thinned budget margins, cut their workforces, cut services, and deferred projects. Revenue diversification in general is one response (Anderson, 1995) state and local governments have to fiscal stress. Diversification occurs when states collect taxes from property, sales, individual incomes, and corporate incomes and generate other revenue. This reduces the government's dependence on one or just a few revenue sources. Another response to fiscal stress is to privatize services (Miniter, 1994), with the dual intent of saving tax dollars and improving service quality. However, Jeffrey Greene's (1996) research found that privatization levels are higher in wealthy, fiscally healthy, suburban cities than in fiscally stressed cities. He reasons that, "Fiscally stressed cities may have too many difficulties coping with their existing situation to introduce a substantial policy change like privatization."

James Ward (2001) found differences between urban governments and rural governments in how they cope with fiscal stress. His research, based on a statewide survey of Louisiana local governments, found urban governments more likely to engage in revenue enhancement strategies, and rural local governments more likely to engage in expenditure reduction strategies. Perhaps this has to do with differences in the opportunities available to them to deal with fiscal stress.

Allen Schick (1988) identified a number of adaptive processes governments (although not necessarily local governments) engage in when faced with fiscal stress. These include cutback budgeting (efforts to reduce spending below the level that would ensue if current policies were continued), the reemphasis of cash budgeting (concern about money spent during the year), efforts to stimulate reallocations of resources (from less important to more pressing needs), program evaluation (systematic review), closer monitoring of budget execution (observe variances and other differences), and the strengthening of financial management (to hold spenders accountable for the costs they incur and the results they produce).

In a recent paper for the Brookings Institution, Pagano (2003) found that cities respond differently to swings in the economy depending on their varying fiscal structures. He found that cities having the authority to tax sales and income generate revenues at a higher rate than do property-tax cities.

CONCLUSION

The fractionating of the literature across many disciplines stems from the different purposes of the writers. Some authors have attempted to instruct or give practical advice to local governments on how to maintain and enhance their fiscal health. Others are more concerned with exploring the concept of fiscal health (and a host of related terms) and the implications of using various definitions for research and practice. Some writers have focused on the measurement of fiscal health. In that, we find numerous perspectives on how best to quantify a local government's fiscal health through various proposed indicators. There is a substantial literature on the factors (independent variables) influencing a government's fiscal health. There are also writings on the influence of fiscal health on other topics of interest to communities.

REFERENCES

Advisory Commission on Intergovernmental Relations. (1973). City Financial Emergencies: The Intergovernmental Dimension. Report A-42. Washington, DC: ACIR.

Alter, T. R., McLaughlin, D. K., and Melniker, N. E. *Analyzing Local Government Fiscal Capacity*, University Park, PA: State University Cooperative Extension Service.

Anderson, J. E. (1995). Fiscal pressures and revenue diversification in the Great Plains. *Business in Nebraska, 50* (598), 1–5.

Badu, Y. A., and Li, S. Y. (1984). Fiscal stress in local government: A case study of the tri-cities in the commonwealth of Virginia. *The Review of Black Political Economy, 17* (2), 91–118.

Bahl, R. (1984). *Financing State and Local Governments in the 1980s.* New York: Oxford University Press.

Bahl, R., and Duncombe, W. (1991). *Economic Growth and Fiscal Planning: New York in the 1990s.* New Brunswick, NJ: Rutgers University, Center for Urban Policy Research.

Bateman, K. R. (1990). Microcomputers and municipal credit analysis Nuveen overall ranking-analysis percentile systems. In T. N. Clark (ed.), *Monitoring Local Governments: How Personal Computers Can Help Systematize Municipal Fiscal Analysis* (41–48). Dubuque, IA: Kendall/Hunt Publishing Company.

Benton, J. E. (1986). Economic considerations and Reagan's new federalism swap proposals. *Publius: The Journal of Federalism, 16* (2), 17–32.

Berne, R., and Schramm, R. (1986). *The Fiscal Analysis of Governments.* Englewood Cliffs, NJ: Prentice-Hall.

Berry, F. S. (1994). Innovation in public management: The adoption of strategic planning. *Public Administration Review, 54,* 322–330.

Brown, K. W. (1993). The ten-point test of financial condition: Toward an easy-to-use assessment tool for smaller cities. *Government Finance Review, 9* (6), 21–26.

Campbell, A. K. (ed.) (1970). *The States and the Urban Crisis.* New York: Columbia University Press.

Ciccarone, R. A. (1990). Building and using a vendor software bad database package for municipal revenue bonds. In T. N. Clark (ed.), *Monitoring Local Governments: How Personal Computers Can Help Systematize Municipal Fiscal Analysis* (55–59). Dubuque, IA: Kendall/Hunt Publishing Company.

Clark, T., and Appleton, L. (1989). Coping in American cities. In S. Clarke (ed.), *Urban Innovation and Autonomy* (31–68). Newbury Park, CA: Sage Publications.

Clark, T., and Chan, J. L. (1990). Monitoring cities: Building an indicator system for municipal analysis. In T. N. Clark (ed.), *Monitoring Local Governments: How Personal Computers Can Help Systematize Municipal Fiscal Analysis* (65–161). Dubuque, IA: Kendall/Hunt Publishing Company.

Dearborn, P. M. (1994). The state-local fiscal outlook from a federal perspective. *Intergovernmental Perspective, 20* (2), 20–23.

Downing, R. G. (1991). Urban county fiscal stress: A survey of public officials' perceptions and government experiences. *Urban Affairs Quarterly, 27*, 314–325.

Finden, R. (1996). GASB finalizing new standard. *American City and County, 111* (11), 8.

Fox, W. F., and Sullivan, P. J. (1978). Fiscal impacts of changes in population for nonmetropolitan areas of the northeast. *Journal of the Northeast Agricultural Economics Council, 7* (1), 41–46.

Gold, S. D. (1992). The federal role in state fiscal stress. *Publius: The Journal of Federalism, 22* (3), 33–47.

Greene, J. D. (1996). Cities and privatization: Examining the effect of fiscal stress, location, and wealth in medium-sized cities. *Policy Studies Journal, 24* (1), 135–144.

Groves, S. M., and Valente, M. G. (1994). *Evaluating Financial Condition: A Handbook for Local Government*, 3rd ed. Washington, DC: International City/County Management Association.

Hembree, H., Shelton, M., and Tyer, C. (2000). Benchmarking and local government reserve funds: theory versus practice. *Public Management, 81* (9), 16–21

Hirsch, W. Z., and Rufolo, A. M. (1990). *Public Finance and Expenditure in a Federal System*, San Diego, CA: Harcourt Brace Jovanovich.

Hoang, H. D. (1990). Personal computer applications for the municipal analyst: an insurance perspective. In T. N. Clark (ed.), *Monitoring Local Governments: How Personal Computers Can Help Systematize Municipal Fiscal Analysis* (65–161). Dubuque, IA: Kendall/Hunt Publishing Company.

Honadle, B. W., and Lloyd-Jones, M. (1998). Analyzing rural local governments' financial condition: An exploratory application of three tools. *Public Budgeting & Finance, 18* (2), 69–86.

Johnson, F. A., and Roswick, D. L. (1991). Local fiscal capacity. In J. E. Peterson and D. R. Strachota (eds.), *Local Government Finance:*

Concepts and Practices (177–198). Chicago, IL: Government Finance Officers Association.

Kleine, R., Kloha, P., and Weissert, C. S. (forthcoming). A new tool for state oversight of local governments' fiscal health. *Government Finance Review.*

Ladd, H. F. (1991). The state aid decision: changes in state aid to local governments, 1982–87. *National Tax Journal, 44,* 477–496.

Ladd, H. F., and Yinger, J. (1989). *America's Ailing Cities: Fiscal Health and the Design of Urban Policy.* Baltimore, MD: Johns Hopkins University Press.

Landis, J. D. (1992). Do growth controls work? A new assessment. *Journal of the American Planning Association, 58,* 489–508.

Lin, W., and Raman, K. K. (1998). The housing value-relevance of governmental accounting information. *Journal of Accounting and Public Policy, 17* (2), 91–118.

Mercer, T., and Gilbert, M. (1996). A financial condition index for Nova Scotia municipalities. *Government Finance Review, 12* (5), 36–38.

Miniter, R. (1994, April 4). Cities privatize for fiscal health. *Insight,* 6–10.

Pagano, M. (2003). City Fiscal Structures and Land Development. A discussion paper prepared for the Brookings Institution Center on Urban and Metropolitan Policy. Washington, DC: The Brookings Institution.

Pagano, M., and Moore, R. J. T. (1985). *Cities and Fiscal Choices: A New Model of Urban Public Investment.* Durham, NC: Duke University Press.

Rattner, Y. (2003). *When Revenues Are Not Sufficient to Cover Growing Expenditures: Understanding How Moody's Evaluates the Financial Position of Local Credits in Times of Fiscal Challenge.* New York: Moody's Investors Service.

Reed, B. J., and Swain, J. W. (1997). *Public Finance Administration.* 2nd ed. Thousand Oaks, CA: Sage Publications.

Reschovsky, A. (1997). Are city fiscal crises on the horizon? Chapter 23 in D. Netzer, and M. P. Drennan, (eds.), *Readings in State and*

Local Public Finance (439–464). Oxford, UK: Blackwell Publishers, Ltd.

Schick, A. (1988). Micro-budgetary adaptations to fiscal stress in industrialized democracies. *Public Administration Review, 48*, 523–533.

Shelton, M. W., and Albee, T. (2000). Financial performance monitoring and customer-oriented government: A case study. *Journal of Public Budgeting, Accounting & Financial Management, 12* (1), 87–105.

Sokolow, A. D., and Honadle, B. W. (1984). How rural local governments budget: The alternatives to executive preparation. *Public Administration Review, 44*, 373–383.

Tschinkel, S. L., and Wall, L. D. (1994). Some lessons from finance for state and local government development programs. *Economic Review—Federal Reserve Bank of Atlanta, 79* (1), 1–10.

Ward, J. D. (2001). Responding to fiscal stress: A state-wide survey of local governments in Louisiana. A research note. *International Journal of Public Administration, 24*, 565–571.

Warner, M. E. (1999). Local government financial capacity and the growing importance of state aid. *Rural Development Perspectives, 13* (3), 27–36.

Wolff, L. W., and Hughes, J. (1998). Net available assets as a proxy for financial condition: A model for measuring and reporting resources available to a local government. *Government Finance Review, 14* (3), 29–33.

Wolman, H. (1992). Urban fiscal stress. *Urban Affairs Quarterly, 27*, 470–482.

THREE
Macro Trends Affecting Local Governments

Local governments are the key service providers of citizens' daily needs. They are charged with designing and implementing complicated and costly policies to protect the public's health, safety, and welfare. Unlike officials of other levels of government, few local leaders, especially in small communities, have been maligned as "faceless bureaucrats" or "never-at-home" politicians. Local officials are often colleagues, friends, neighbors, or acquaintances of those they serve. Face-to-face interaction must be maintained with citizens, especially in dealing with controversial issues, such as housing and zoning.

This chapter examines the macro trends that continue to affect the changing local political, social, and economic environment. The trends discussion presented in this chapter was previously published (Cigler, 1996, 1989) and has been condensed here. All of the macro trends reviewed have financial implications for local governments, but Chapter 4 is used to examine financial trends, especially state-local financial relations and attempts to increase local financing options. This is followed by Chapter 5, which provides examples of using expenditure reduction options as one way to increase fiscal health.

Many of the trends are largely beyond the control of individual local governments, as outlined in Figure 1.1 and the related discussion in Chapter 1. However, municipal and county associations that represent local government interests often exert considerable influence over national and state actions that affect local government. If local government officials are aware of these "macro" trends, they can at least adapt to them, if not influence or change them. The examples of local adaptation that are presented in Chapters 4 and 5, which look at both financing and expenditure options, are supplemented by an eight-point strategy for achieving local governmental fiscal health presented in Chapter 9.

The macro trends in the local government environment that are discussed in this chapter have evolved over several decades. They include not only demographic, economic, and social dynamics, but also increased complexity of problems and demands for service in a time of regionalization, uneven resources, and the role of citizen trust and participation. As suggested in Figure 1.2, public policies and local managerial and fiscal operations should anticipate and influence foreseeable changes affecting government. Local governments, more than in the past, must learn to work within an overall governance system that includes the public, private, and nonprofit sectors working together on policy making and service delivery issues. Local government officials must play coordinator and facilitator roles within the governance system, as well as maintain appropriate control over service delivery by the nongovernment sectors. As such, local officials must also know how to write and monitor good contracts with private and nonprofit service deliverers.

DEMOGRAPHIC AND SOCIAL TRENDS

The long-term fiscal health of local government is framed in large part by demographic, economic, and social trends. A changing population that includes more elderly in need of long-term care, more youth in schools, more youth prone to crime, and a more diverse workforce lacking in basic skills are key demographic trends influencing local governments. The number of senior citizens in the United States will increase by more than 60 percent over the next two decades; the population of seniors 85 years and older will more than double (Hughes, 1992). The fastest growing age group—seniors over 75 years old—increases demand for costly long-term health care, nursing homes, transportation services, recreation, and law enforcement. This increased demand may not be as costly if older workers work longer than in the past, continue to be wealthier than in the past, and accumulate more assets.

School enrollment is growing more rapidly than at any time since the baby boom of the 1950s and 1960s, with growth generally concentrated in outer-ring metropolitan suburbs where new classroom construction is required. Costly government programs for health care, primary and secondary schools, and colleges strain government budgets. National and state mandates and preemptions increase local government costs, as do rising public salaries and employee benefits. High standards for performance challenge the balancing of quality and affordability. Infrastructure costs— for aging schools, highways, and bridges, as well as for expansion to the suburbs—must include funding for an expansion of the telecommunications infrastructure.

According to census data, by the end of the 1980s, 90 percent of U.S. population growth and 87 percent of employment growth occurred in metropolitan areas (i.e., cities and suburbs). More than half of all Americans now live in a little more than three dozen metropolitan areas and about a third of the population lives in central cities. The U.S. population is becoming more diverse in its racial and ethnic composition, with disproportionate numbers of minorities lacking the skills necessary for the increasingly service- and information-based economy. Spatially, minorities are now majorities in the largest central cities.

The 2000 census results show that some large cities experienced population gains in the previous decade. New York City, for example, had more than 8 million people for the first time in history. A key factor in the urban revival in some places through the 1990s was a steep decline in crime, especially violent crime. The dominant U.S. population trend, however, continues to be a decentralization of economic and residential life, not a return to core cities, which generally continue to lose ground to their suburbs as well as rapidly developing new communities on the far fringes of metro areas (Katz and Lang, 2003; Frey, 2003; Lang, 2002).

The 2000 census also shows that suburbs of America's 100 largest metropolitan areas grew more than twice as fast as their central cities during the 1990s, a pattern that held for all types of cities whether the total population was dropping, stagnating, or growing. The fastest growing cities in the 1990s were in the West. Their combined population rose by over 15 percent during the decade, although that still lagged behind the growth of their suburbs (21 percent). The South had the fastest expanding suburbs, with suburban population in that region increasing by 26 percent during the decade, far outpacing the 11 percent growth in southern cities' population. Northeastern and midwestern cities grew much more slowly and many suffered declines. Still, their suburbs prospered. Midwestern cities, for example, netted a collective population increase of just 186,000 people in the 1990s (with nearly half showing declines), but their suburbs gained 2.9 million new residents. Two-thirds of the cities in the Northeast lost residents in the 1990s, but New York City and Boston showed significant population gains. The central and southern New Jersey metropolitan areas, entirely suburban in character, were the fastest growing metropolitan areas in the Northeast in the decade (Berube and Forman, 2002).

Within the differing regional patterns of growth and decline, all types of households in all parts of the United States choose to live in suburbs more than in cities. Even childless and single-person households are attracted to suburbs more than to cities.

Many immigrants now bypass the cities altogether. Racial and ethnic minorities, which were 19 percent of the suburban population in 1990, were 25 percent of the suburban population by the end of the decade. Jobs have traveled with the people. In America's 100 largest metropolitan areas, only 22 percent of all people work within 3 miles of the city center. More than 60 percent of the regional employment in such cities as Chicago, Atlanta, and Detroit is located more than 10 miles from the city center (Orfield, 2002, 1996).

Overall U.S. population growth is slowing. Future household formations will not match the baby boom–generated explosion that occurred between 1970 and 1980. But as more Americans move into middle age, the end of the period for raising families and buying houses, the demographic implications for local government are profound. Metropolitan disparities exacerbate and escalate demand for services and the physical infrastructures that support them. Central cities continue to house the nation's very poor. Although urban poverty rates have fallen, the 2000 census shows that they remain twice as high as suburban poverty rates. Heavy welfare caseloads continue to burden distressed cities.

Jargowsky's (1997) analysis of neighborhood poverty showed a doubling in the 1970s and 1980s of people living in areas of concentrated poverty (i.e., areas with poverty rates of 40 or more). His analysis of the 2000 census data, however, showed a reversal in the 1990s (Jargowsky, 2003). His national analysis of high-poverty neighborhoods and the concentration of poor individuals in those neighborhoods in the 1990s and 2000 shows that the number of people living in high-poverty neighborhoods declined by 24 percent or 2.5 million people in the 1990s. That improvement stands in contrast to the 1970–1990 period in which the high-poverty neighborhood population doubled. Jargowky found the steepest declines in midwestern and southern high-poverty neighborhoods. He also found that concentrated poverty declined among all racial and ethnic groups, especially African

Americans. Specifically, the share of poor black individuals living in high-poverty neighborhoods declined from 30 percent in 1990 to 19 percent in 2000. The number of high-poverty neighborhoods declined in rural areas and central cities, but suburbs experienced almost no change. In fact, some older, inner-ring suburbs around major metropolitan areas experienced increases in poverty, but the rates generally remain well below 40 percent. The dramatic improvement in the 1990s in concentrated poverty may not be a permanent trend. The national economic downturn in the early twenty-first century and the declining status of many older suburbs suggest that public policies will need to be responsive to low-income families.

Baby "boomlets," especially in the suburbs, lead to rising school enrollments. Racial and ethnic diversity, sometimes accompanied by insufficient parental incomes, generates fiscal stress for local areas with underdeveloped educational infrastructures. The shrinkage in the 18- to 34-year-old demographic group adversely affects the production of entry-level housing, the availability of new entrants into the labor force, and any economic activities predicated on the availability of young adults.

Another important demographic trend is the heterogeneous nature of American immigration patterns, whether to cities or to suburbs. While a quarter of foreign-born immigrants live in just three cities—Los Angeles, New York, and Chicago—there has been an increase in immigrants to all parts of the nation and within metropolitan areas. The immigrants differ in national origin, settlement patterns, language ability, and economic status. These characteristics pose unique challenges at the local level, especially in times of economic downturn and as related to the immigrant population in post 9/11 America (Massey, 1998; Singer, 2003).

The competitive strategies many cities pursued during the 1990s, such as sports stadium building, hotel construction, and downtown revitalization, are often seen less as the "ticket" to economic vitality than is dealing with basic needs such as good schools and safe neighborhoods, competitive taxes, efficient services, and a viable real estate market. People choose to live where these amenities exist and businesses want to invest there. City-specific "solutions" are giving way to broader efforts to slow metropolitan decentralization and to promote urban reinvestment. Many older suburbs, for example, face the same types of challenges that have long challenged cities. Rapidly developing suburbs are learning that sudden growth brings the unanticipated costs of traffic congestion and overcrowded schools. Forging new alliances among communities within a metropolitan region on issues such as infrastructure spending, reinvestment, and affordable housing is again on the metropolitan agenda (Katz and Lang, 2003; Katz, 1998).

Service sector restructuring aimed at becoming more adept at information processing requires more highly skilled workers. The increasingly service- and information processes-based U.S. economy makes local tax systems less responsive to economic growth than in the past because of the difficulties of taxing services. The economic term used to describe the tax system as not growing with the economy is inelasticity.

Property taxes, the primary local revenue source, are not popular, and unfunded mandates from the national and state governments continue to increase the local fiscal burden. Legal decisions about the use of the property tax to pay for schools also place burdens on local governments to find new ways to finance services. Demands for increased services by the elderly, often at the expense of other programs, coupled with resistance to tax increases or changes in the Social Security system, place significant burdens on local governments in determining the appropriate mix of services and how to fund them. The post 9/11 local environment places additional burdens on funding first responders such as police, fire and emergency services workers, as well as the public health community. The national recession in the early twenty-first century helped to create state budget deficits (e.g., due to the drop in sales and income tax revenues), affecting the national government's and the states' ability to offer local government assistance.

TELECOMMUNICATIONS INFRASTRUCTURE, TECHNOLOGY, AND THE GLOBAL ECONOMY

Local governments operate in a global economy that requires dramatic changes in the way those governments operate. Connections are easier to make across large distances; the Internet and other communication technologies have a leveling effect by making it possible for more local governments to compete economically as equals. Even small, rural communities can have successful economic development strategies in a global economy if they can utilize an appropriate mix of other factors, such as telecommunications and other technologies. Broadband is becoming an essential infrastructure, just as highways and water and sewer utilities have been.

The emergence of so many new actors on the global stage suggests that organizations, including local governments that traditionally were competitors, must now work as partners and form working alliances. Still, the globalization of trade affects the local corporate tax base. And the economic clustering of related firms is advocated for community and regional economic development.

The costs of providing the full array of telecommunications to rural areas are often prohibitive, widening the gaps in service availability between rural areas and urban areas. A similar gap in technology occurs across wealthy urban neighborhoods and poor urban neighborhoods. An information-based economy that is fueled by advanced telecommunications may mean that small cities and rural areas—many already with declining population and job bases—lose locational advantages derived from proximity to railroads or water. These "places without purpose" (in an economic sense) often struggle for survival.

Advances in technology, especially the ability to collect, store, and retrieve information from a central database, have a significant impact on government operations. Technology holds promise for cost savings across a wide variety of policy and service delivery areas. It is a catalyst for procurement reform, which enhances the possibility for more state-local and county-municipal piggybacking of governmental purchases. Resources can be catalogued and linked, and "paperless" offices can facilitate the use of single applications for state aid and other transactions. Business assistance applications can be consolidated and transferred through electronic mail; information clearinghouses are more accessible. Local employees have increased access to training, information, and each other. Costly geographic information systems (GIS) and computer-assisted design graphics can be developed jointly with other municipalities for a wide variety of local planning functions.

Technology poses an array of financial challenges for local governments. Gambling on the Internet (cybergambling), for example, could increase the use of new types of tax shelters, greater gambling addiction, and possibly more regulations. These would have impacts on local government tax bases, spending for social problems, and compliance with regulations. E-commerce taxation issues are an additional concern. State and local governments want the authority to tax Internet sales and services the same as they tax sales in stores.

Institutional and Policy Fragmentation

Government entities—municipalities, townships, counties, school and other special districts—number more than 83,000 nationwide according to 2000 census data. Although the individuals in this local "nonsystem" are relatively autonomous, they all draw on the same fiscal base. Service delivery and policy-making responsibilities are not integrated and are largely separated from the realities of metropolitan economic organization. The multiplicity of local governments results in uneven resources. As such, local areas are fraught with financial and social inequality.

The growth corridors of metropolitan areas in our decentralized economy are the "edge cities" of the metropolitan rim and perimeter areas where much of the job creation and residential construction took place beginning in the 1980s (Garreau, 1991; Lang, 2002). Deindustrialization and disinvestment had devastating financial consequences for the urban core. Since the mid-1990s, there has been a resurgence of interest in the rebuilding and revitalizing of inner cities, for example, through infill strategies and the redevelopment of previously abandoned industrial or "brownfield" sites.

Local public policies and management efforts have developed largely through piecemeal processes, often born of expediency. Today there is also a multiplicity of policy leaders. No longer is elected position necessarily the dominant source of policy ideas. Leadership and new ideas can come from anyone. This multi-centered-policy dominance, along with the multiplicity of local governments and the governmental and institutional fragmentation, calls for new kinds of leadership. Specifically, bold, focused, and accountable political leadership that uses facilitative styles of management (Cigler, 1990; Svara, 1994; Chrislip and Larson, 1994) is increasingly being recognized as necessary. An array of formal and informal governance structures collaboratively deal with the problems of achieving coordination at the local level. As mentioned earlier, attention has shifted from solely vertical relations (e.g., national-state-local) toward horizontal relations among local (intermunicipal) governments.

More than 90 percent of municipal governments in the United States serve communities of less than 10,000 people; more than

80 percent of them serve fewer than 5,000 people. More than three-fourths of county governments serve populations less than 50,000 (Schenker, 1986; Cigler, 1996; Census, 2000). Nearly one-third of the U.S. population lives in rural areas, and approximately two-thirds of all governmental units exist there. Although most people live in urban areas, most local governments, both inside and outside metropolitan areas, serve small populations and have limited management capacity and small in-house professional staff (Honadle, 1983, 1981; Cigler, 1993a, 1991). Yet many citizens prefer the Jeffersonian-like qualities of small governments in which they personally know their officials, and small governments may be well suited to areas that need a limited type and/or amount of services.

Small governments, which lack slack in their budgets, have less flexibility to respond to fiscal constraints than do larger municipalities. They are unable to eliminate the delivery of basic public services such as police, fire, water, and street and sewer construction and maintenance. Thus, existing service levels are difficult to maintain when revenue losses are experienced. There are also fewer management personnel available for coping with an array of challenges and fewer revenue options available to officials (Cigler, 1991, 1986).

The diversity of local government types increases the fragmentation of the local system. More than 3,000 U.S. counties serve as the key delivery units for health, welfare, transportation, and educational services; some large counties have assumed the characteristics of regional governments. Special districts, excluding those for education, continue to proliferate (now numbering nearly 29,000) due to their territorial flexibility and political popularity; this poses significant accountability challenges (Burns, 1994; Foster, 1997; Miller, 2002). Regional councils are entrepreneurial in their provision of services to local governments, often serving as facilitators of regional policy development and service delivery approaches.

State authority patterns give local governments varying ability to control their own future, with local taxation and borrowing authority sometimes limited by constitutional and statutory restrictions. Here, too, dramatic changes are occurring. Managerial and fiscal capacity building efforts strengthen local governance processes. Some states have offered mandate flexibility to help local governments, including more flexibility to municipalities' ability to diversify their revenue sources. Capacity building assistance—for undertaking evaluation and reporting, benchmarking, and strategic planning—is available in some states. System-changing options, once rarely even discussed, are now of growing interest and there are a growing number of success stories. These include local government restructuring through revenue and/or tax base sharing, greater accountability of special districts, and the transfer of powers from municipalities to their county and/or state (Cigler, 1993b). These topics are discussed in more depth in Chapter 4.

INCREASED PROBLEM COMPLEXITY

Old problems have not died; they have changed their form and/or grown worse. Illegal drugs heavily drive crime rates. The feminization of poverty places large numbers of women and children at risk. Entire families face homelessness. As technology improves, health care and education costs for governments rise because of the high cost of equipment and the new services made possible.

In dealing with complex problems, local officials struggle with ways to integrate services, including linkages with state and other agencies. Policy options must be clustered and linked: Employment requirements and day care, education and job training, child and maternal health—all go together in effective welfare reform. Natural resource management, economic development, and environmental problems require regional solutions involving many government entities, too. However, this can blur lines of responsibility, leaving the sense that "when everyone is in charge, no one is in charge" (Cigler, 1990, p. 646). The challenges of moving toward decentralized, cooperative, and collaborative problem solving are immense in the working partnerships between and among local governments, states, and other entities. Strategies, structures, and systems for each policy area must be reshaped. Fiscal considerations obviously become more complex when there are more actors and connections.

Air pollution, inadequate water and sewers, solid and hazardous waste disposal, and lingering toxic wastes are regional problems. But we do not have a nation of regional citizens and support for regional problem solving is in its infancy. The fiscal means to deal with problems on a regional basis—and with the support of a regional citizenry—is a largely unmet challenge.

Serious imbalances between fiscal needs and resources grow as income inequalities escalate. By 1990, for example, the wealthiest one-fifth of the nation's citizens made more than the other four-fifths combined. Reich (1990) argued that the rich retreat into their own self-sufficient communities, which he calls the "secession of the successful." Disparities—between suburbs and cities, whites and minorities, private wants and public good—are wide and still evident in the 2000 census data. Analyses demonstrate, however, that the well-being of the nation and its local governments are intertwined (e.g., see Rusk, 1993; Barnes and Ledebur, 1994; Downs, 1994; Cisneros, 1993). Central cities benefit from their well-off suburbs; suburban areas flourish more when their central cities do well.

Interjurisdictional competition (of population, investment, external aid) within metropolitan areas jeopardizes the revenue bases of many governmental entities and redistributes wealth within regions, causing both inequity and inefficiency. Local debt levels have increased, especially in poorer areas. This is one factor in the demand for capital-intensive services and the preference for more government services.

INCREASED DEMAND FOR SERVICES

Local governments provide traditional and basic services but cannot borrow their way out of problems. Public demands for activism, growth, and innovation continue unabated despite antigovernment rhetoric and aversion to taxes. Growing service demand; the increasing scope, range, and costs of services; and the tax limitation movement have pushed local (and state) governments to reconsider what they do, how they do it, and with what resources. Local government structural reform is receiving renewed attention, including tax-base and revenue-base sharing options. In addition, a skeptical citizenry has pushed elected officials to embrace new management paradigms, alternative policy tools, and service delivery options, including financing options. This changes the mix of service deliverers and modifies governments' relationships with service recipients.

Numerous alternative ways to deliver services (e.g., intergovernmental agreements, contracting with the private sector, and user fees) limit the scope and form of direct public activity and necessitate different public and private management styles. Decisions about which services to provide are increasingly separated from actual service delivery. Service providers come from all sectors; this places local governments increasingly in facilitative roles. The changed environment includes greater competition within local governments and among sectors, the development of standards and performance measures, greater attention to mission- and goal-driven tasks, and greater attention to prevention, not treatment. Many local governments no longer simply spend—they "earn," through a variety of entrepreneurial activities. Local managers not only must do it right; they must convince others that everything was done right. Government officials have a large tool bag of innovative, proactive, risk-taking strategies for balancing the needs of bureaucracy and the democracy bureaucracy serves. The flip side of increased flexibility, however, is an increased demand by citizens for accountability. This means that local officials must be results-oriented and must measure and report performance more than in the past.

Increased Citizen, Group, and Elected Official Activism

Recipients of local services are more empowered, both individually and collectively, than in the past. The Internet, for example, has increased citizens' ability to be more active in all phases of the policy process and has increased expectations of government performance. Local officials can more easily than in the past assess citizen interest systematically, both before and after service delivery. Generally, citizens now have more mechanisms for representation in the policy process, for example, alternative dispute resolution, small claims court, and citizen advisory panels. They also have more access to every phase of the policy cycle, ranging from problem identification, agenda setting, policy formulation, policy and program implementation, to evaluation.

Increased citizen activism puts more pressure on local elected officials to demand greater accountability from public agencies, sometimes leading to micromanagement. Similarly, state legislators are prone to view local governments as "just another interest group" (Cigler 1995, 1994) and to tighten their regulatory grip in some matters, especially fiscal. Institutional responsibilities are fragmented, blurred, and diffused, making access easier for special interests. The media have amassed enormous influence in designing agendas. Citizen customers of local government services have often redefined their wants as "needs" and their needs as "rights." In that milieu, local officials must work harder to educate citizens and to achieve a balance of matching rights with responsibilities (Cigler, 1995–1996). Satisfaction of the "customer" by service delivery agencies becomes more difficult, frustrating everyone. The increased citizen activism makes the job of the local official, whether elected or appointed, more complex and time-consuming.

Local government is expected to be open, accessible, and responsible to its citizens. Citizen expectations may be "louder" than in the past, but they are not fundamentally new. The needs, versus resources dilemma must be understood within the context of a governance system in which citizens are not widely engaged in the civic discovery and meaningful participation. As mentioned earlier, individual and group "wants" in recent years have been self-redefined as "needs" and then demanded as "rights," with little or no engagement in the broader discussion about what is good for society. Single-issue advocacy, hostility, confrontation, and a general lack of civility often overshadow the development of what has been called the civic infrastructure, civic culture, or social capital deemed necessary for collectively analyzing, understanding, and responding to public problems (Harwood, 1991; Putnam, 1993; Peirce, 1993; Rusk, 1993; Cisneros, 1993; Downs, 1994). Collaborative processes and other new ways of interacting are a growing part of local officials' environment. This is increasingly so for examining alternative service delivery options and their financing.

INCREASED INTEREST IN REGIONAL ISSUES

Regionalization of services is driven by economies of scale and promoted by national and state mandates. Police forces, solid waste disposal, and emergency services were becoming regionalized by the mid-1990s. Water, sewer, and storm water systems are prime candidates for regionalization in the early twenty-first century. In other cases, municipal funding and/or responsibilities have shifted upward to counties or the state. State regulatory functions (e.g., environmental regulations) may also be shifted to regions. Municipal functions such as fire fighting may be consolidated within regions. Planning may be directed to the regional level. Rural areas especially sometimes engage in multi-community collaboration—partnerships involving two or more communities across sectors—for economic development and other activities (Cigler, 2001, 1999).

The emerging regionalism places local governments in a pivotal role in dealing with issues that cross political boundaries: transportation, law enforcement, environmental concerns, public health, education, social services, and so on. The consequences of poor judgment often have a cumulative impact, and some policy decisions are irreversible. Changes in the local environment occur simultaneously in the social, economic, technological, political, and physical domains. Flexible, adaptive, and creative managerial strategies—including fiscal strategies—are needed to respond continuously to change.

With an increasingly dynamic, open, and competitive world economy, governments have developed new ways of working with the private sector to improve economic performance. Companies think in terms of economic regions and industry clusters, not political-geographic jurisdictions. Local governments are challenged to develop regional relationships within a political system organized around individual places—towns, townships, boroughs, cities, and counties—to achieve economic development. The challenge is to develop a regional citizenry without destroying the strong feelings of community at the local level (Barnes and Ledebur, 1994).

LOOMING STRUCTURAL BUDGET GAPS

Municipal governments deal with issues of life and death (police, corrections, fire protection, public health, emergency management) and those related to lifestyle (housing, land use, zoning, schools), and they provide other basic services (streets, lights) and amenities (libraries, parks). Counties are the major providers of human services in the public sector, serving as the administrative arms of states to implement many state and national programs. Special districts and public authorities play important roles in providing water and sewer systems, parking garages, housing, parks, and other services.

By the end of the 1980s, the national deficit hampered the ability of governments at all levels to create jobs, protect the social safety net, and counter the detrimental effects of deindustrialization that were transforming many metropolitan areas. Still today, cities' fiscal ills transcend class, racial, and jurisdictional boundaries; rural areas mirror the metropolitan problems, with additional obstacles posed by isolation, low population density, and less revenue flexibility, among other differences (Honadle, 2001, 1993, 1983).

In the mid-1990s, the states were financially healthy as a result of a strong national economy. Demographic trends, however, resulted in rising bills for costly services. The demands were met by staggering amounts of state spending for the escalating costs of health care (driven by Medicaid costs); corrections (rising incarceration rates, mandatory sentencing, court mandates on prison overcrowding); primary and secondary education (due to a baby "boomlet"); higher education (new technology, the growing need for financial aid); and local government aid, especially after devolution. State spending grew significantly through workload increases (such as increased caseloads and school enrollments) and inflation, new and expanded programs (in education, resources, and health-related areas, primarily), tax relief, and a variety of other programs (spending related to federal mandates, local fiscal relief, spending related to court cases). State economies were so strong that most states reduced taxes. Many states also set aside rainy day funds—reserve accounts funded during an economic expansion as a defense against declining revenues and rising need for public services in a recession.

The stability of most state and local government budgets for most of the 1990s was only short-term because a national recession began in Spring 2001. Rising unemployment, mounting job losses, slowing personal income growth, and a sharp falloff in capital gains and stock options led to state revenues falling well short of expectations. Revenues for most states were well below projections by mid-2002 and in many states they actually declined from the previous year. State expenditure needs, conversely, increased as a result of the economic hardships caused by job losses. The terrorist attacks on September 11, 2001, placed new spending demands on state budgets in the areas of public safety and public health. Between 2001 and 2002 Medicaid spending rose sharply, just part of a steep national increase in health care costs. As long as the national government offers no solutions, Medicaid costs continue to threaten everything else in state budgets, including education, transportation and aid to local governments.

Data available on the web sites of the National Governors' Association (*www.nga.org*) and the National Association of State Budget Officers (*www.nasbo.org*) show that in May 2002 state budgets were in the worst shape in 20 years. Thirty-nine states cut their projected budgets by a total of $15 billion in 2002 and overall spending rose only 2 percent in fiscal 2002, with an increase of only 1.4 percent expected in fiscal 2003. The figures do not cover the costs of inflation and population growth. Even with an economic recovery, the short-term future looks very tough fiscally.

Revenues in 48 of the 50 states were below estimates in fiscal 2002, often by wide margins. Thirty-six states had already planned or implemented cuts in public services by the end of 2001. Because state revenues historically lag 12 to 18 months behind the first signs of economic recovery, fiscal 2003 was worse than fiscal 2002. Minimally, that is because the states have already exhausted their one-time options as they patched together budgets. The states dipped deeply into their rainy day funds in late 2001 and through 2002, with the states that fared worse being those that had not built strong rainy day funds in the 1990s. Many states used funds received in settling lawsuits with the tobacco companies or tapped public employee pension funds to meet state constitutional requirements that they balance their budgets. As such, year-end balances were two-thirds smaller than they were just two year earlier—barely 3.5 percent of expenditures.

It is likely that annual excesses of expenditures over revenues will persist well beyond 2003, absent corrective actions. While rainy day funds provide a way to maintain programs during a cyclical economic downturn, in some states the fiscal situation is a combination of cyclical problems and structural problems. If rainy day funds were used to compensate for structural budget deficits—long-term imbalances between the growth rate of revenue and the growth in the cost of basic programs—those states will face even more severe fiscal problems.

State governments began to rethink their spending priorities and how to make changes after 2001, with significant impacts on local governments. A wide array of spending-related options were examined: eliminating or modifying programs; suspending or reducing cost-of-living allowances; spending deferrals (e.g., post-poning some capital projects); shifting funding from the general fund to other sources, such as fees, other governments, and the private sector; program improvements and efficiencies, for example, through restructuring, consolidation, or improved management; and reverting or disencumber funds when possible.

Revenue-related options also ran the gamut: eliminating or modifying tax expenditures, broadening basic tax bases, raising tax rates, transferring special fund balances, improving tax compliance and collections, accrual revisions, and asset sales. Since the early 1990s, every state has changed its tax code in some way, typically by raising taxes in response to tight fiscal conditions early in the 1990s and then cutting taxes in the middle and late 1990s and into 2000 and early 2001. Tax relief, however, tended to focus on higher-income families, including reductions of corporate income taxes and estate taxes.

Some of the more notable state activities in 2002 that affect local economies and revenue were raising the tax on cigarettes, abolishing some mandatory sentencing for crimes, and requiring collaboration among local governments as a condition of aid. Lacking cash due to slumping sales tax revenues and especially rising Medicaid costs, some states withheld millions in tax reimbursements from local, especially county, governments. In 2002 and 2003, some states cut local revenue-sharing dollars to balance their budgets and other states proposed to do so in the future. Local governments were left few options and will likely have to make politically unpopular choices, such as tax increases or program cuts.

The terrorist attacks in the United States on September 11, 2001, led to increased state and local concern and spending on homeland security and emergency management. In addition, a decline in air travel and tourism disproportionately affected cities and urban residents, given the central role of convention centers, hotels, and restaurants. Without significant changes in government operations—and better control of spending—states and their local communities will have financial difficulties in the near future. If current demographic trends hold, there will be slower income growth and an increase in the number of youth, elderly, and others using government services. The size of the local budget gap will be determined in part by the levels of national and state government funding in the near term and whether a major recession occurs and how long it lasts. If the states are eventually permitted to tax Internet purchases, that might affect state aid to local governments. The local budget gap is also affected by whether local governments pursue new revenue options (e.g., by eliminating unproductive business incentive programs, using optional sales taxes, revising tax exemption laws, and increasing user fees) and by other state and local responses to dramatic changes in their environment (such as 9/11 and the increased spending for homeland security). State aid to local government has been growing more slowly than other areas of state spending. By 1992, state aid amounted to 32.3 percent of state spending, which was the lowest proportion since the U.S. Census Bureau began reporting the statistic in 1956 (Gold, 1995) and the trend has continued into the twenty-first century.

CONCLUSION

Local governments will look different in the future—and there may be fewer general-purpose local governments (although special-purpose governments may continue to proliferate). Greater use of a variety of alternative service delivery mechanisms means that local governments will focus more on results, not on processes. They will need to be more concerned than ever about financing, monitoring, and evaluating. The "big questions" about local governments and their relationships with other governments and sectors involve who should do what, when, where, why, and how. These are highly contentious topics and the future is uncertain. Local government is in a long-term trend toward more professionalization of their management, technical, and financial responsibilities. As such, the types of financial tools presented in this book should contribute to improved capability for dealing with the myriad of challenges facing local officials.

DISCUSSION QUESTIONS

1. Select at least three macro trends affecting local government and discuss their implications for your hometown.

2.   Based on the trends discussion in this chapter, what type
of actions do you think your leaders should pursue?

REFERENCES

Barnes, W. R., and Ledebur, L. C. (1994). *The U.S. Common Market of Local Economic Regions.* Washington, DC: National League of Cities.

Berube, A., and Forman, B. (2002). Living on the Edge: Decentralization within Cities in the 1990s. Washington, DC: Brookings Institution, October.

Burns, N. (1994). *The Formation of American Local Governments: Private Values in Public Institutions.* New York: Oxford University Press.

Chrislip, D. D., and Larson, C. E. (1994). *Collaborative Leadership: How Citizens and Civic Leaders Can Make a Difference.* San Francisco, CA: Jossey-Bass.

Cigler, B. A. (2001). Multiorganization, multisector, and multicommunity organizations: Setting the research agenda, in M. P. Mandell (ed.), *Getting Results Through Collaboration: Networks and Network Structures for Public Policy and Management,* Westport, CT: Quorum Books, 71–85.

———. (1999). Pre-conditions for the emergence of multicommunity collaborative organizations, *Policy Studies Review, 16* (1), 86–102.

———. (1996). Adjusting to changing expectations at the local level. In J. Perry (ed.), *Handbook of Public Administration,* 2nd. ed. San Francisco, CA: Jossey-Bass, 60–76.

———. (1995). Just another special interest: the intergovernmental lobby. In A. C. Cigler and B. Loomis (eds.), *Interest group politics,* 4th ed., Washington, DC: Congressional Quarterly Press, 131–153.

———. (1995–96). Governance in the "re–ing decade of the 1990s," *The Public Manager, 24* (3), 3.

———. (1994). The county-state connection: A national study of associations of counties, *Public Administration Review, 54* (1) (January/February), 3–11.

———. (1993a). Meeting growing challenges of rural local governments, *Rural Development Perspectives*, *9* (1) (Fall), 35–39.

———. (1993b). State-local relations: A need for reinvention? *Intergovernmental Perspective*, *19* (Winter), 15–18.

———. (1991). The special problems of rural county governments. In D. Berman (ed.), *County Government in an Era of Change*, Westport, CT: Greenwood Press, 90–106.

———. (1990). Public administration and the paradox of professionalization, *Public Administration Review*, *50* (6) (November/December), 637–653.

———. (1986). Small city capacity-building and the new federalism. In J. A. Stever and L. Bender (eds.), *Administering the New Federalism*. Boulder, CO: Westview Press, 160–181.

Cisneros, H. G. (ed.) (1993). *Interwoven Destinies: Cities and the Nation*. New York: Norton.

Downs, A. (1994). *New Visions for Metropolitan America*. Washington, DC: Brookings Institution.

Foster, K. A. (1997). *The Political Economy of Special-Purpose Government*. Washington, DC: Georgetown University.

Frey, W. H. (2003). Boomers and Seniors in the Suburbs: Aging Patterns in Census 2000. Washington, DC: Brookings Institution, February.

Garreau, J. (1991). *Edge City: Life on the New Frontier*. New York: Doubleday.

Gold, S. D. (1992). The federal role in state fiscal stress. *Publius: The Journal of Federalism 22* (Summer), 33–47.

Harwood, R. (1991). *Citizens and Politics: The View from Main Street America*. Dayton, OH: Kettering Foundation.

Honadle, B. W. (2001). Rural development policy in the United States: Revisiting the cargo cult mentality. *Journal of Regional Analysis & Policy*, *31* (2), 93–108.

———. (1993). Rural development policy: Breaking the cargo cult mentality. *Economic Development Quarterly*, *7* (3), 227–236.

———. (1983). *Public administration in rural areas and small jurisdictions: A guide to the literature.* New York: Garland Publishing Company.

———. (1981). A capacity-building framework: A search for concept and purpose. *Public Administration Review, 41* (5), 575–580.

Hughes, J. W. (1992). Demographic and Economic Parameters: The National Framework. Paper presented at The future of small cities: Pennsylvania conference. Easton, PA: Lafayette College (November 5–6).

Jargowsky, P. A. (2003). Stunning Progress, Hidden Problems: The Dramatic Decline of Concentrated Poverty in the 1990s. Washington, DC: Brookings Institution, May.

———. (1997). *Poverty and Place: Ghettos, Barrios, and the American City.* New York: Russell Sage Foundation.

Katz, B. J. (1998). Reviving Cities: Think Metropolitan. Washington, DC: Brookings Institution, June.

Katz, B. J., and Lang, R. E. (eds.) (2003). *Redefining Urban and Suburban America: Evidence from Census 2000.* Washington, DC: Brookings Institution Press.

Lang, R. E. (2002). *Edgeless Cities: Explaining the Elusive Metropolis.* Washington, DC: Brookings Institution Press.

Massey, D. et al. (1998). *Worlds in Motion: International Migration at the End of the Millennium.* New York: Oxford University Press.

Miller, D. Y. (2002). *The Regional Governing of Metropolitan America.* Boulder, CO: Westview Press.

Orfield, M. (2002). *American Metropolitics: The New Suburban Reality.* Washington, DC: Brookings Institution Press.

———. (1996). *Metropolitics: A Regional Agenda for Community and Stability.* Washington, DC: Brookings Institution Press.

Peirce, N. R. (1993). *Citistates: How Urban America Can Prosper in a Competitive World.* Washington, DC: Seven Locks Press.

Putnam, R. D. (1993). *Making Democracy Work: Civic Tradition in Modern Italy.* Princeton, NJ: Princeton University Press.

Reich, R. (1990). *The Work of Nations.* New York: Random House.

Rusk, D. (1993). *Cities Without Suburbs.* Washington, DC: Woodrow Wilson Center Press.

Schenker, A. (1986). Zero employment governments: Survival in the tiniest towns. *Small Town, 16,* 4–11.

Singer, A. (2003). At Home in the Nation's Capital: Immigrant Trends in Metropolitan Washington. Washington, DC: Brookings Institution, June.

Svara, J. (1994). *Facilitative Leadership in Local Government: Lessons from Successful Mayors' Chairpersons.* San Francisco, CA: Jossey-Bass.

FOUR
Financing Trends and Options

The formal nature of the state-local relationship has historically been unitary and hierarchical (i.e., vertical). Local governments, whether general-purpose towns, boroughs, townships, cities, or counties, are primarily creatures of the states; they are treated legally as municipal corporations. States generally curb their status by providing for some limited municipal immunity through home rule, but state government remains dominant and home rule makes no claims about separate spheres of state and local authority. Home rule is instead an umbrella of policies and understandings between a state and its local governments. In recent years, however, there has been some shifting on the mix of functions and responsibilities among government types.

This chapter focuses on the local governments' response to the changing macroenvironment, especially fiscal issues. The chapter begins with a preliminary discussion of the state-local fiscal relationship and briefly summarizes local revenue sources, commonly called revenue streams, such as those derived from traditional sources (e.g., the property tax). A key focus is on state-local revenue diversification options and their policy effects, as well as the factors related to local finance that influence fiscal capacity and flexibility. Chapter 5 then examines a variety of alternative service delivery (ASD) mechanisms that can be used by local governments to enhance their fiscal situation. Some guidelines for selected ASD options are provided. Throughout both chapters, particular attention is paid to the state-local fiscal relationship because of the constitutional status of local governments. Put simply, they are not mentioned in the U.S. Constitution; they are created by states and states give them their powers and responsibilities. This chapter examines fiscal federalism and a series of revenue diversification options. It is condensed from a series of publications on local government structure, fiscal federalism, and revenue diversification (Cigler, 1997, 1996, 1993a), with updates and additions cited where appropriate.

FISCAL FEDERALISM

Local governments generally possess substantial power in the regulatory arena and have extensive regulatory and service delivery responsibilities. The most significant constraint on municipal power is in fiscal matters. Mixed with the great diversity of local governments in type, function, size, wealth, and demographics (age, race, income, and class) is interjurisdictional competition that results in a pattern of fiscal disparities in service delivery and social inequities across metropolitan areas and between rural and urban places. Local land use and growth management practices, often of an exclusionary nature, deepen the extent of local fiscal disparities.

Preemption is the most common form of state control over municipal taxing power; that is, state legislatures often deny their municipalities the power either to impose a particular tax or to impose a tax on a particular class of taxpayers. Extensive state legislative limits on revenue raising and expenditure powers, along with tight limits on alternative sources of revenue, are usually more restrictive than state restraints on local regulatory powers.

One state-local fiscal trend is increased state judicial activism regarding local fiscal disparities. Court orders have responded to local prison overcrowding, child welfare program deficiencies, and the lack of access to legal counsel and quality of representation for juveniles. After years of favoring local autonomy in cases of school finance inequities, recent state court decisions (e.g., Montana, Kentucky, Ohio, and Texas) have invalidated local school financing systems. A similar narrowing of local autonomy has occurred through recent state court cases involving charges of exclusionary zoning. Courts in California, New York, New Jersey, and Pennsylvania, for example, have dealt with differences in interlocal wealth by linking housing policies to regional general welfare concepts. Fair share affordable housing is promoted in some states.

School finance and exclusionary zoning exemplify the call for a greater state role (including supervision of local governments) and a need for more local accountability in projecting "reasonableness" into policies regarding housing, zoning, land use, and educational financing issues. Increasingly, relationships among the states and their local governments impact local responsibilities and financing.

The transition to more block grant programs in the American political system means that states will largely determine the success of national block grants, based on how they treat cities and counties. As more responsibilities are devolved from the national government to state and local governments, the concern is for the efficiency of service delivery. Block grants remove the countercyclical thrust of traditional welfare programs. They are fixed in size, whereas entitlement spending increases with demand, which typically rises in economic recessions.

Increased regulatory flexibility by both the national government and state governments imposes increased costs on local governments. With flexibility comes greater concern for accountability. Benchmarking, the development of performance standards, performance measurement, and reporting all help increase accountability but are costly. In addition, shifts away from command and control through the heavy hand of regulation generally lead to greater use of incentives. Incentives, however, burden local governments with lost revenues. The use of local enterprise zones, for example, may spur economic development in the long term, but provide either no tax revenue or less tax revenues to the sponsoring government in the short term. Other relaxed regulations offer local flexibility to spend funds, meaning that there is a greater local need for expertise in deciding on funding options. Economic efficiency, benefit-cost analysis, risk assessment, performance measurement, and accountability are part of the flexibility-accountability package.

SIZE OF GOVERNMENT

State and local governments employed 15.4 million "full-time equivalent" workers in 2001, a 2 percent increase over 2000, according to the Commerce Department's Census Bureau. Of that total, according to the 2001 Annual Survey of State and Local Government Employment and Payroll, found at the Census Bureau web site (*http://www.census.gov/govs/www/apesstl.html*), local governments reported 11.2 million full-time equivalent employees. It is at the state and local levels that government employment is rising much faster than nondefense employment in the national government. This is because state and local governments are the primary deliverers of services in the American political system and devolution has increased in recent decades.

Periodically updated information found on the web sites of the National Conference of State Legislatures (*www.ncsl.org*) and the National Association of State Budget Officers (*www.nasbo.org*) depicting the components of total state spending (general fund plus earmarked funds) reflect the service delivery role: elementary and secondary education, 22.5 percent; Medicaid, 19.5 percent; higher education, 10.9 percent; transportation, 8.8 percent; corrections, 3.8 percent; public assistance, 2.4 percent; and all other expenditures, 32.1 percent (numbers may not add due to rounding). Components of state spending in the general fund (i.e., primarily discretionary spending of revenues derived from general sources and not earmarked for a specific item) are elementary and secondary education, 35.7 percent; Medicaid, 14.4 percent; higher education, 12.2 percent; corrections, 7.0 percent; public assistance, 2.5 percent; transportation, 0.9 percent; and all other expenditures, 27.3 percent (numbers may not add due to rounding). Despite the dominance of elementary and secondary education in state spending, Medicaid, the means-tested entitlement program funded by the states and the national government, has been the second largest component of state spending, both from general funds and from all spending sources since fiscal 1993. It is also the fastest growing part of state budgets.

Tabulations from the Census Bureau's 2001 Annual Survey of State and Local Government Employment and Payroll show that most full-time equivalent employees worked in education (8 million), hospitals (922,000), and police protection (885,000). Other employment categories are corrections, streets and highways, public welfare, health, judicial-legal, financial administration, and fire protection. In 1996, for example, local governments raised or charged $508 billion and received another $271 billion in intergovernmental aid from the states and national government.

About two-thirds of local government revenues are collected by assessing a tax, charging a fee, or relying on some other type of locally raised money. Most local tax revenues are from the property tax, but local governments also make substantial use of user fees or charges, and many use sales and/or income taxes. In contrast to their "own-source" revenues, local governments also receive intergovernmental transfers, (i.e., national and state aid). This area, however, has changed the most over recent decades in the local revenue mix. The 1960s and 1970s were characterized by increasing involvement of the national government in the direct financing of local government in response to what was perceived as an urban crisis. From the 1960s to the early 1980s, the direct national involvement with local governments spanned the Great Society and its War on Poverty and General Revenue Sharing, in which local governments received annual formula-driven funds. In 1982, nearly a quarter of federal aid to state and local governments went to local governments.

The mid-1980s saw a period of national retrenchment in aid to local governments that continues today. By 1996, local governments received 11 percent of total national government distribution to state and local governments. While national government aid to local governments grew slowly, it increased substantially to state governments. Importantly, despite the shift away from direct aid to local governments, the national government's aid as a percentage of total state and local tax revenues has remained relatively constant.

Local governments are the primary deliverers of services. In 1996, for example, they spent $1.52 for every dollar spent by state governments in service delivery. States concentrate nearly two-thirds of their spending on education and social services. Local government spending is more diverse, although education is the greatest expenditure category and is incurred not by general-purpose local governments, but by school districts, a type of special or single-purpose government. In 1996, local education spending accounted for 37.6 percent of local government expenditures. Social services were the next largest expenditure, accounting for about 12 percent of expenditures. A little less than a third of local government expenditures are made in such traditional property-related services as utilities (water, sewer, and energy), environmental and community development, public safety, and transportation. The category of local government administration represents fewer than 5 percent of total local government expenditures. However, this category may represent a much higher share of expenditure for individual units of government, particularly in small communities.

The decentralization of fiscal federalism since the late 1970s, along with an increase in state and local governments' responsibilities, has increased the complexity of local governments' relationships with other levels of government and the private and nonprofit sectors. The devolution of responsibilities began against the backdrop of tax revolts, beginning in California in the 1970s with Proposition 13, and was followed by state limitations on local governments' fiscal discretion. The full brunt of significant federal disengagement in local affairs was first felt in the 1980s, when states abandoned their own tax- and spending-control initiatives and state and local governments often engaged in competitive practices to finance their activities.

The private investment–public disinvestment philosophy and programs of the Reagan administration in the 1980s (Cigler, 1990) quickened the pace of devolution, helping fuel the states' resurgence by redirecting intergovernmental fiscal policy. In the late 1970s and throughout most of the 1980s, state and local resiliency in the face of the "three R's" revolt of taxpayers, recessions, and reduction in aid flows (Shannon, 1990) was noteworthy. While relatively successful in the "three E's" economy, efficiency, and effectiveness local governments have had more difficulty in handling questions of equity and justice, sometimes resulting in costly lawsuits and programs. For example, environmental justice lawsuits arise when minorities in a community think that a disproportionate amount of "LULUs" (Locally Unwanted Land Uses) occur in their community or neighborhood.

Beginning in the 1980s, local governments had to adjust to challenges that required greater sophistication and skills due to dramatic economic, demographic, technological, ideological, and political changes. The long-term intergovernmental centralizing trend that began in the 1930s was somewhat redirected by a devolution of many programs and regulations from the national government to state and local governments, dramatically changed the local fiscal environment. Since the 1980s, there has been attention to a sorting out process based on a rethinking of the respective responsibilities of national, state, and local governments and of the private and nonprofit sectors. Local governments have attempted to respond to the crosscurrents of centralization (due to unfunded mandates and regulations from the national government and the states), decrementalism (gradually reducing or eliminating some programs), decentralization (being given more administrative authority), deregulation (in some cases), and devolution (Cigler, 1989, 1993a; Honadle, 2001).

All of these challenges continue in the early twenty-first century. The current emphasis on homeland security and what has been labeled the war on terrorism have furthered the sorting out process. There are more national resources going to national defense than in the recent past and more funds dedicated to securing the homeland (e.g., smallpox vaccines, airport surveillance, and emergency management), with fewer funds available for traditional domestic priorities. This trend burdens local governments to provide own-source revenues for service provision without increased financial aid from higher levels of government.

The changing political fiscal environment since the 1980s forced local officials to become more self-reliant and this trend continues. Dwindling assistance from other levels of government and continued demand for governmental spending at all levels has led to a rethinking of fiscal practices at the local level. This includes somewhat of a shift in financial ties from the previous dominant vertical federalism (i.e., national-state-local) to greater concern for building horizontal federalism (e.g., municipal-municipal, county-county) in the form of partnerships with other communities and with the private sector.

Emerging changes in the form of governmental activity have led to a different local political environment, which has affected local fiscal circumstances, activities, and options. Known as third-party government, government by proxy, or, more narrowly, privatization, intermediaries between local governments and citizens are often responsible for actually producing goods or services. That is, third parties, such as nonprofit agencies, have replaced, in many cases, the direct administration of programs by government (Savas, 2000; Hodge, 2000). In 2002, the mayor of Boston announced plans to ask hospitals, colleges, and museums to offer such services as scholarships and mentoring to the city in an effort to offset shrinking municipal revenues. As such, these nonprofit institutions, which do not pay property taxes in many states, would contribute the services in addition to annual payments they have made in lieu of taxes since the 1970s. The services contribution concept, however, cannot account for large amounts of a municipal budget gap.

Local governments carry out many national and state policies, and local governments themselves contract with the private sector or not-for-profit organizations. The local administrator's environment, then, is a fluctuating one, which crosses over from the public sector to the private sector to the nonprofit sector. Governance, not just government, and intersector, not just intergovernmental relations, are the realities of the local environment in which public sector officials play facilitative and coordinative roles.

Local Response to the Macro Trends

What are local governments doing to meet their responsibilities in light of the trends discussed in Chapter 3 and the state-local realities regarding fiscal federalism discussed previously? Cigler (1998) used data from telephone interviews with six officials in each state who work with agencies that attempt to build local government capacity to outline several operating principles that define the local response to the macro trends examined in this chapter and in Chapter 3. This section of the chapter is condensed from that emerging trends research.

Local officials are reassessing the rationale for local government action. This results in a wide array of alternative ways to deliver services, all of which must be examined closely for their fiscal soundness and operational effectiveness. Privatization, for both the production and the delivery of services, and outsourcing of government operations (payroll, ticket processing, bill collection, prison administration) are examples. This is especially problematic when delivering, measuring, and monitoring human services, such as juvenile and family services, some welfare activities, home care, and nursing homes. Privatization reduces the number of local employees and the ratio of government employees to the total population. It requires improved standards, performance contracts, and monitoring for results.

Privatization remains a highly contentious issue, facing frequent opposition by unions and the courts. *Privatization* itself is sometimes less an issue than increased *competition* in the public sector. Competitive bidding, for example, is being required for local governments in the provision of public services. Low bids are less important than altering overall costs. When public agencies must compete with the private sector for contracts, cost efficiencies and service effectiveness can be achieved.

Flexibility, choice, and discretion in the use of policy instruments are also more prevalent than in the past. Market-oriented approaches, such as vouchers, user charges, contracting out, and demand reduction are part of the policy tool kit available to local officials. Centralized, rule-bound, inflexible, and process-oriented approaches are giving way to decentralization, flexibility, and cost-effective approaches to allocation and management of finances. The financing and delivery of services is driven more by consumers, not programs, making local governments work with others (e.g., states, each other, counties) to analyze needs.

The national government and the states are less direct funders, service providers, and regulators than in the past. Instead, they are more facilitators, catalysts, enablers, convenors, information generators and disseminators, standard setters, brokers, and capacity builders in helping to develop new relationships among people and groups across all sectors and government levels. This means that local governments rely more on their own revenue generation, have increased responsibilities, and also must form new relationships.

A number of states, for example, are less likely to offer grant programs to a single jurisdiction and are more likely to reward jurisdictions that collaborate. Local officials must take advantage of the important state activities in building the managerial, financial, and technical capacity of their local governments. States often disseminate information on "best practices" or "model" policies; devise measurement, monitoring, and evaluation systems; and otherwise facilitate continuous learning by partnering with local entities. An example of a capacity-building technique by a state for its local governments is a circuit-rider program in which assistance is offered to a cluster of local governments for financial management, economic development, or other local functions.

Many state programs offer financial incentives combined with sanctions to change the behavior of local governments. An example is the use of cash rewards to schools that improve students' academic performance, coupled with the imposition of penalties on schools that do not improve. Penalties include teacher probation, firing of principals, or turning control over the school to the state.

Comprehensive or holistic approaches to complex and intertwined problems must be forged, based on the complexity of problems, fiscal constraints, and accelerated changes in technology and communication. Global competitiveness has pushed the public sector toward boundary-spanning roles in building relationships for the development of self-sufficient regional economies. This includes holistic approaches to workforce skill development, high-quality physical infrastructure development, strategic and visionary collaborative planning, leveraged financial and technical resources, and adequate provision of the basics for quality living (e.g., affordable, quality health care and housing). Intergovernmental and intersector collaboration are necessary in all of these areas.

Traditionally, local governments have participated in economic development wars, spurring intense interjurisdictional competition through the use of extensive tax abatements and other incentive packages to lure businesses. These policies are based on the belief that growth will reduce local unemployment, build the local tax base, and provide a favorable business climate that will increase prosperity. However, growth often necessitates increased outlays for public infrastructure (roads, sewers, water, schools). This can drain a municipality's finances if the development does not pay the full costs of expanded facilities and services and pits localities within a region against each other.

Newer approaches involve the public sector's attempting to increase participation by the private sector in developing coherent economic development policies and helping to avoid unproductive jurisdictional competition. These public-private partnerships work to ensure that business needs are understood and met and that long-range strategies are implemented despite turnover among elected officials. Local entrepreneurial strategies often involve increased emphasis on cooperation with employers to foster skills needed in the workplace. School-to-work and school-to-career programs link local schools and employers before students reach the workforce. Local governments and states are working together, in addition, to facilitate the role that communication technologies, such as distance learning and telemedicine, play in improving the quality of life, especially in rural areas.

Very broad approaches to economic development and policy are occurring in the twenty-first century. These include innovative, private sector–oriented strategies that are responsive to small and medium-sized businesses, the key providers of jobs, by helping to increase the businesses' productive capacity through technology transfer and assistance and help in marketing, financing, and general management. The strategies also include inducing greater industry diversification to lessen the risk associated with reliance on one or a few businesses, addressing the deterioration of labor market conditions for low-income individuals by increasing the number of and access to employment opportunities; investing in neighborhoods (e.g., community-based planning, community economic development); and promoting regional solutions to regional problems (e.g., workforce development through regional partnerships within industry sectors and transportation, land use, air and water quality, recreation, and labor demand and supply issues). Promoting sound fiscal practices is a precondition for responding to the needs of the economy, including rationalizing tax policy.

Regional delivery of goods and services is becoming more common. A key question is whether states will mandate regional approaches or develop incentive-based systems to spur local collaboration. Some states (e.g., Connecticut) have tried to abolish counties and to create regional units. In other states, the push is to strengthen counties, especially their planning authority. New units and boundaries may emerge for regional entities in some parts of the United States, such as those based on watersheds. Financing techniques growing in popularity are a regional assets tax and various forms of tax-base and revenue-base sharing. An example of an assets tax might be a countywide tax for parks and recreation, such as that used by Allegheny County, Pennsylvania, in the Pittsburgh region. A popular state incentive is to reward municipalities that regionalize services with more points in grant competition for state funding.

Another trend involves attempts to counter the negative effects of urban sprawl. State concurrency legislation, for example, requires that no local development take place unless services such as roads, sewer, solid waste disposal, parks and recreation, education, and health care are provided at the same time. To accomplish this, local governments are empowered to set standards for each service and to prohibit development unless the requirements are met. Communities can agree to provide the services, or developers can provide them or post bonds to ensure that the necessary infrastructure and services are provided as development takes place.

Entities that supply services to the public are increasingly expected to operate at the community level, either individually or collectively. This requires local governments to improve the capacity of governing and advisory boards, for example, through training. Issues of accountability, eligibility, and liability necessarily receive increased attention as local service delivery responsibilities expand.

Accountability for performance, including strategic planning processes, benchmarking, performance monitoring, and consultative processes with citizens are being increasingly stressed over processes and inputs. Similarly, greater attention is being paid to impact analysis, risk assessment, user design, and information disclosure to citizens.

LOCAL REVENUE SOURCES

As local officials face the macro trends discussed in this chapter and in Chapter 3, they must be aware of local revenue sources and options for increasing a local government's revenue flexibility all within the limits of the state-local relationship. The remaining sections of this chapter address these issues and are condensed primarily from Cigler (1996, 1993a), with the major works of others noted in the publications cited here.

A local government's fiscal capacity and flexibility depend on the appropriateness, variety, and productivity of its revenue sources. Flexibility results from having authority over revenue sources that can be varied in response to new and changing demands for services. Extensive use of earmarked taxes, charges, or special assessments and tightly drawn tax bases reduce fiscal flexibility. Whether local governments need more revenues or should have more revenue flexibility is less an issue than are questions about the appropriate mix of revenues for financing services and meeting policy-making responsibilities in an equitable manner. Questions about who pays what and how, to which level of government, and for what services are fundamental to determining fairness in the cost of public service provision.

Intergovernmental fiscal transfers are an important source of local revenues, although such transfers have declined in recent years. Intergovernmental funding between local government and state or national agencies either requires a percentage match by the local government or is formula-based, in theory increasing funding as the demand for mandated services increases. In practice, funding is often capped by appropriation, so that an increase in required services is not always accompanied by greater funding. This is especially the case for county government. Mandates to provide service on demand strain local delivery systems and consume additional revenues. Many local governments aggressively and often successfully pursue court remedies to recoup tax dollars spent in support of mandates. In the process, however, the local government loses interest earnings and the ability to use funds for other purposes.

The intergovernmental fiscal relationships between and among local government and the federal and state governments differ and have changed over time. Until national general revenue sharing was abolished in 1986, local governments received extensive national funding. They continue to receive block and categorical grants that must be spent for specific purposes and usually require a matching contribution. Smaller governments, for example, are eligible for community development block grants, used primarily to expand economic opportunities for low- or moderate-income persons. The events associated with the September 11, 2001, terrorist attacks led to new funding for first responders such as emergency medical personnel and the fire and police services, as well as public health agencies, among other agencies.

State aid for local governments varies widely across states and can be used for general or specific purposes. Some states have assumed funding responsibility for functions formerly handled by local governments (e.g., welfare). Some of the differences depend on the responsibilities of counties compared to other forms of local government. Counties have responsibility for education in several states (e.g., North Carolina, Maryland, and Tennessee). Counties assume most human services spending and responsibilities but some states do not mandate county involvement in providing public health, hospitals, corrections, or public welfare.

Property taxes, both real and personal, comprise the largest single source of local own-source revenue. Despite some changes in property tax finances, they will likely continue to be the largest source of funding for operations. Since the tax limitation movement of the late 1970s and 1980s, actions by state and local governments have diversified local revenue bases. Property taxes still constitute most of local tax revenues, a dependence that has remained constant for several decades. It may be that the continued strength of property taxes is the result of improved assessment practices and the use of circuit breakers to make the tax less regressive.

The use of property taxes varies widely by type of local government, however. For example, independent school districts receive most all of their tax revenues from property taxes and counties receive nearly 75 percent of the tax revenues from that source. Municipalities, however, receive approximately only half of their tax revenues from the property tax. There is wide variation among states in the use of local property taxes. Most low-use states are in the South and the West and high-use states tend to be in the North and the Northeast.

Despite its drawbacks, the property tax has many advantages. It provides a stable source of revenue; taxes nonresident property owners who benefit from local services; finances property-related services such as police and fire protection and the construction of infrastructure such as streets, curbs, sidewalks, and storm drainage systems; is difficult to evade, making collection and enforcement relatively easy; and enables local governments to achieve autonomy from the national and state governments (Bland, 1989). Still, paying for education with property taxes poses significant equity issues.

Other revenue sources include user charges at airports, recreation, and rental facilities; fees (e.g., via courts, wills, sheriffs); miscellaneous receipts; and national and state grants and reimbursement for expenditures for some mandated social services (e.g., county programs for the mentally disabled, controlled substance abusers, neglected and abused children, and the chronically ill and elderly). Licenses, permits, fines, and forfeitures are fairly static revenues and change only through state legislation. Miscellaneous receipts are usually onetime-only or minor revenues. Local governments also receive interest earnings.

REGIONAL SPRAWL AND LOCAL FINANCES

Sprawl is the land use pattern characterized by low-density or uneven physical development occurring at the fringe of an urbanized area. Regional sprawl results from individual, business, and community land use decisions generally supported by public subsidies for roads, sewers, waterlines, tax breaks on mortgages and is often facilitated by a transportation system that includes affordable personal vehicles, low fuel prices, excellent roads, and free parking at work and shopping destinations. The urban fringe attracts development due to the widespread availability of and access to open space, lower-density development that permits higher return on investment, quality education in school districts in developing areas that are financially advantaged by the new tax base, and perceptions of a better quality of life than in higher-density urban areas.

The explicit revenue implications of the linkage between the property tax and sprawl are vague, but public finance plays a significant role in shaping metropolitan growth patterns. This is primarily because use of the property tax by assorted jurisdictions represents the dominant factor in a region's public financial structure, local government fragmentation, and the fact that much of the growth that occurs in a region, especially one that is slow-growing, is actually an intraregional redistribution of households and commercial and industrial development. Reliance on the property tax results in a service-delivery system that depends heavily on a community's tax base. Developing communities must aggressively seek growth, especially commercial and industrial growth that requires fewer community services than residential development, to ensure the resources necessary for service provision. Tax base competition gives jurisdictions strong financial incentives to try to zone out poor people. When fringe growth occurs simultaneously with the abandonment of older urban communities, the revenue bases of the older communities shrink, thus causing service cuts and making older communities even less able to compete for the growth and development necessary to support essential services.

The movement of residents and businesses outward within a metropolitan area thus has two anticipated effects. First, the movement within a metropolitan area drains its economic vitality and results in additional disinvestment in the urban center. The resulting tax base shrinkage reduces the ability of older communities to repair, maintain, and operate existing infrastructure, such as storm water and sanitary sewers. At the same time, continued outward growth means that the region must keep investing public funds in construction of a new infrastructure even though the existing infrastructure is underutilized. The second effect is an intraregional redistribution of the local jurisdictions' tax base.

Since the late 1970s, grants, loans, and revenue-sharing assistance from the national and state governments to help underwrite infrastructure costs have been either eliminated or have dwindled, as have targeted resources to older communities (for housing, education, transportation, job training, etc.) to help adjust for regional inequities. In addition, new rules and regulations applied to local governments often place new responsibilities on them without providing funds for implementation. The Environmental Protection Agency (EPA), for example, has mandated the elimination of combined sewer overflow systems, a major source of water pollution.

INTERGOVERNMENTAL ASSISTANCE

In addition to urban sprawl, the increased reliance by local governments on alternative revenue sources has been spurred by the decentralization of fiscal federalism since the late 1970s. This trend was fueled by the mix of such factors as federal disengagement, the tax limitation movement, recessions, deficits, and demographic trends. These trends are not likely to change quickly and there is an ever-increasing reliance on local governments. The use of intergovernmental assistance to facilitate local delivery also means decreased flexibility of revenue. In addition, state laws generally require that local budgets, especially county budgets, be balanced, making budgeting processes largely revenue-driven. Available revenues determine the level of spending for any given year (Bland, 1989; Gosling, 1992).

Local governments share fiscal, service-delivery, and policy-making responsibilities with states and other local governments. The alternatives available to them in meeting their responsibilities are difficult: expenditure reduction, which reduces the level and/or type of services provided to citizens; increasing tax rates on current sources of revenue at a time when citizens have expressed dissatisfaction with the property and other taxes; borrowing at a time when debt is already high (Bahl and Duncombe, 1993); and/or finding new sources of revenue, including the adoption of new taxes or charges for service, as well as tax base changes: The last category is the most difficult to accomplish because some type of state action is generally required.

For example, the state role in local governments for diversifying their revenues is crucial. States can draw on five broad options to increase the revenue flexibility of their local governments, as explained by Cigler (1996):

1.   Changing the level or pattern of intergovernmental assistance;

2.   Altering local tax options;

3.   Revising the property tax laws and their administration;

4.   Altering user charges or fees; and

5.   Encouraging or mandating a fundamental restructuring of the system of local governance, which includes linking planning and land use powers to opportunities for intergovernmental cooperation that ultimately enhance county revenues.

Each of these options is examined in some depth here. It must be remembered, however, that it is often difficult for the states to facilitate local revenue flexibility. As explained in Chapter 3, many state revenue structures are currently weak. In the short run, this is the result of a national recession, but it is primarily the effect of increases in Medicaid, corrections spending, and rising school enrollments that have helped produce structural state deficits that began in the 1990s but were not widely recognized as "structural" (e.g., linked to changing demographics such as rising Medicaid costs) until about 2002.

CHANGING PATTERNS OF STATE ASSISTANCE

It is unlikely that hard-pressed states will allocate significantly greater resources to their local governments. Some states are reexamining their patterns of aid and making attempts to provide more targeted assistance by changing distribution formulas and/or the conditions of assistance, as well as monitoring state aid. Other sources of state revenue gasoline taxes, so-called sin taxes on tobacco products and alcohol, a sales tax on selected services, and/or lottery proceeds can be shared with general-purpose local governments. In 2002, many states, however, increased cigarette taxes to deal with their own budget deficits and did not pass on more money to their localities. Sorting out issues in the federal system, such as state assumption of increased financial responsibility for courts and poverty-related activities (e.g., indigent health care and cash welfare assistance) were not addressed.

Another area where state policies have affected local revenue flexibility is the targeting of local support for urban redevelopment. Enterprise zones were adopted by state and local officials, beginning in the 1980s, to spur investment and job creation in specified geographic areas by means of relaxed government controls and tax incentives. Eligibility requirements, selection processes, and incentives vary but include tax credits; reductions or abatements on sales, materials, inventory, or property taxes; job training or employer tax credits; management and technical assistance and related earmarked services; and increased public services in the zones. These policies both directly (through decreased revenues) and indirectly (through reliance on traditional tax structures) decrease local government flexibility (Bartik, 1991).

LOCAL TAX OPTIONS

Increased local taxation authority through statutory constitutional provision offers the greatest prospect for achieving revenue flexibility. But what options should be considered? How should the various options be evaluated? Public finance defines criteria for "good taxes," which commonly:

- Raise the desired amount of revenue;
- Are considered fair, based on equity standards such as the ability to pay;
- Have reasonable administrative and compliance costs; and
- Do not create economic inefficiency by causing serious distortions in markets (Aronson, 1985; Musgrave and Musgrave, 1984).

Good taxes also offer stability to the local revenue system.

In addition to these criteria, a general thrust for tax reform is toward a broader base and lower, less intrusive rates. County option sales taxes, for example, were in place in 31 states by 1987 (USACIR, 1989) and are used by one-third of all counties—including all counties in 10 states (Todd, 1991). Virginia and California have a universal local sales tax at a mandated rate—in effect, a state tax that is shared with localities based on point of sale, thus minimizing distortions in locational choice within those states and lowering governmental administrative costs as well as retailers' compliance costs. Florida's 1986 attempt to expand the base of its sales tax highlights a problem. Florida tried to include consumer and business services, such as legal and advertising services, but legal and legislative challenges resulted in a repeal of the law.

The major source of untapped local tax revenue is a local-option income tax, which is usually allowable if no local-option sales tax is in effect. Three types of local income taxes can be authorized: a full-fledged tax such as a state income tax administered by local units; a local income tax piggybacked on a state income tax and collected by a state; and a locally administered payroll tax (Liner, 1992). Such a payroll tax, levied at a single flat rate, is the major local income-tax option. This tax is usually collected by payroll withholding, with no exemptions, deductions, or filing of tax returns, thereby affording ease of government administration and low taxpayer compliance costs. However, the cost to employers, especially small businesses, can be high.

Some municipalities use local income taxes, such as in many municipalities in Pennsylvania. Local-option sales and income taxes have some negative features, such as large rate differentials and differences in base definition. Local-option taxes can be collected by the county but are often collected by the state (to circumvent problems of uneven administration and enforcement) and disbursed to the local governments or counties after some portion of the amount collected is paid to the state to defray the costs of administration. The piggyback income tax is based on either adjusted gross income or state tax liability, thereby minimizing the administrative costs to the locality and the compliance costs to taxpayers. The piggyback income tax, in addition, uses a broader income base than the payroll type of income tax and can allow for exemptions and deductions (Knapp and Fox, 1992). Liner (1992) argues that a piggyback local income tax could be made to have the same degree of progressivity as the most progressive state income tax and that it is paid only by residents of the jurisdiction that levies the tax. This conforms to a benefits-received principle of taxation (i.e., those who benefit from a public service should bear the costs) and the burden of supporting a public service should be distributed in proportion to the amount of use or benefit received from the service. The progressive nature of the tax, within a jurisdiction, is consistent with the ability-to-pay principle.

Conversely, as Liner points out, a payroll tax is regressive because it is derived solely from wages, the key or only source of a low-income taxpayer's earnings. Payroll taxes also violate another commonly accepted principle of tax fairness and equity, the ability-to-pay principle, which asserts that taxes should be levied in accordance with taxpayers' ability to pay. Specifically, the payroll tax violates the subordinate concept of horizontal equity (i.e., those with the same ability to pay should pay the same amount in taxes). Families that receive all of their income from wages are taxed on all of their income via a payroll tax. Families that receive all of their income from interest or dividends, for example, bear no tax burden (Liner, 1992).

Other alternative taxes include alcoholic beverage excise taxes, tobacco products taxes, severance taxes, insurance premium taxes, business and occupation taxes, hotel-motel or occupancy taxes, and real estate transfer taxes. In some places, these taxes can be applied only in unincorporated areas and they often have restrictions on use of the revenues and how the levies must occur. For example, a percentage of the revenue from a hotel-motel tax might be earmarked for promoting tourism, conventions, and trade shows. Depending on design and earmarking principles, in addition, these taxes may violate the benefits-received and ability-to-pay principles of tax fairness (Mikesell, 1995).

Option taxes are generally earmarked for specific purposes and require voter approval. Both factors limit flexibility. Most states continue to specify which jurisdictions can levy a tax, what the taxes can be used for, and how the levies must occur. Several safeguards should be considered when designing and implementing local nonproperty taxes: a uniform tax base, state administration, universal or widespread coverage, a constrained rate option, and state equalization. Basic information on the status of state and local attentiveness to these safeguards is lacking. The latter safeguard, it must be noted, is most suitable to discussions of tax sharing and state aid, which are discussed elsewhere in this chapter. In some states, state laws give incorporated towns the right to preempt certain nonproperty taxes. While such laws provide municipalities with stable and predictable sources of revenue and guard against excessive taxation of residents and businesses, county governments are hurt.

PROPERTY TAX REVISIONS AND IMPROVED ADMINISTRATION

Local government revenue must be maintained at a steady flow to support the continuous and uninterrupted provision of public services. Sales and income taxes should be elastic, to grow with the economy. A recession, for example, decreases revenue yields. Elastic revenues are important to include in a tax system, but stable revenue sources, such as the property tax and user charges and fees that do not fluctuate automatically with changes in the economy, are fundamental. Yields from stable revenue sources change primarily when the rate is altered, although population growth and zoning changes from residential to commercial affect tax yields. Also, user charges and fees vary with the use of a facility or activity (e.g., zoo visitations and building permits). An appropriate mix of stable and elastic revenue sources maintains the necessary balance in the public finance system to adequately support local activities.

The property tax remains the most important local tax (Aronson and Hilley, 1986), especially for school districts and counties. For general-purpose governments (i.e., municipal governments), there is a growing trend toward lessening reliance on the property tax and moving toward a more diversified revenue system. When considering the use of various revenue sources to achieve revenue adequacy and stability, reliance by local governments on the property tax clearly must be addressed carefully. Real property is immobile, and property taxes are productive. It has been argued that property taxes are less regressive than previously thought and less regressive than some of the alternative taxes that are promoted (Bowman, MacManus, and Mikesell, 1992). Property taxes are unpopular, although not widely perceived as unfair. As Liner (1992) suggests, factors related to the payment of the property tax may account for its unpopularity. Payment is due in a lump sum or twice per year (although people with mortgages usually make monthly payments to an escrow account). Tax liabilities are not tied to income, so retired residents on fixed incomes are liable for increased taxes. Reassessments can increase the tax liability suddenly and substantially.

Bowman, MacManus, and Mikesell (1992) reviewed research that found that increased access to diversified revenue might have some negative effects. An overall increase in tax effort in a metropolitan area may negatively affect overall employment growth. The authors argue that sophisticated research on the locational decisions of firms shows that tax uniformity or neutrality tends to promote efficiency, suggesting that more research is needed to examine the degree to which activity is affected and the sensitivity of the effect to different tax provisions. Ladd (1992) confirmed the presence of tax mimicking for total local tax burdens and for property tax burdens in a study of large U.S. counties: local governments take into account the tax burdens in other jurisdictions when making their own tax decisions.

A number of changes geared toward broadening the property tax base are available for generating additional local revenues. New criteria for identifying and exempting from taxation property used for purely charitable purposes can be developed. In the search for new revenues, municipalities often challenge the tax-exempt status of nonprofit hospitals, educational institutions, and similar organizations. State constitutions and assessment laws generally do not include a comprehensive definition of a purely public charity, so these cases are being decided by the courts. States can also remove restrictions that exempt state property from local property taxes, including the provision of in-lieu-of-tax payments provided by the state to local jurisdictions.

The ability to use tax increment financing (TIF) is a common municipal financing tool. TIF districts, in which specified funds are raised to finance public improvements, are created by earmarking part of the regularly assessed property taxes. No additional fees are collected from property owners, and the TIF districts remain part of the local government. TIF offers a visible link between those who pay for infrastructure and the construction, but it depends on potential development and uses the same millage rates for an entire jurisdiction.

Serious problems in administering the property tax persist (Mields, 1993). Governments often fail to meet statutory requirements to maintain current market values through timely property reassessments. Some states fail to implement improvements in administration, valuation, and collection and computer technology that would help achieve progressivity (Rourk, 1993).

To improve the fairness of property taxes, some states have established grant programs for local governments to reassess valuations of real property, and some states require annual valuations. States can provide assistance to local governments in establishing assessment standards, maintaining data for county assessors, training assessors, and updating and computerizing assessment systems. A state can correct unfairness in tax laws by separating the appeals function from the local tax administration function.

States can also permit taxing jurisdictions to target property tax relief, which can affect homeowners exclusively (i.e., a homestead exclusion) or all property owners (i.e., a universal exclusion) through reductions of a given amount in the market value of the property. Circuit breaker laws can protect the elderly or others from having to pay more than a set percentage of their income in property taxes.

USER CHARGES AND FEES

Nontax revenues are moving toward a greater variety in the types of user charges and fees imposed by local governments for services. The use of service charges and fees allows a relatively tight linkage between service provision and the costs of the service (i.e., the benefits principle is upheld.) If the demand for a particular service is not widespread and/or if the beneficiaries can be identified and given benefits denied to nonpayers, user-charge financing is desirable. Charges and fees, however, sometimes can be regressive.

Services for which user fees have been charged include water, sewage disposal, parking fees, bridge and highway tolls, garbage collection, and recreation. Care must be taken so that low-income persons are not adversely affected by user-charge systems. Building permit and inspection fees can be charged to help defray the cost of building code enforcement. Traffic and parking fines, forfeitures of money posted to guarantee appearance in court, and court fees and costs also provide revenue, as do license fees to cover the cost of regulation. User fees enhance access to capital markets because a flow of revenue is guaranteed. It is typical for a city, notes Thomas (1991), to generate 70 percent of its revenue from non-property-tax sources.

An administrative challenge associated with user charges is the difficulty of true pricing of public services. Proprietary funds include enterprise funds and internal service funds (ISFs). The former account for the financing of self-supporting activities that sell services to the general public; the latter account for the financing of services (e.g., data processing, vehicle maintenance) provided by one agency to another agency and supplied on a cost-reimbursement or charge-back basis (Chang and Freeman, 1991).

There is an important relationship between efficient provision of internal services and the quality of the services delivered to the public (Ukeles, 1982), but little is known about the use and operation of ISFs in the public sector (Coe and O'Sullivan, 1993; Chang and Freeman, 1991). ISFs can form the basis for the accurate pricing of user fees and service fees (Downing, 1992; Netzer, 1992). Coe and O'Sullivan found that cities used ISFs for pricing services, facilitating equipment replacement, and making contracting-out decisions. Chang (1987) found that governments might not be fully recovering depreciation through user fees. Leonard (1986) argued that a major contributor to undermaintenance of infrastructure is that government entities do not recognize ongoing depreciation expenses.

An emerging user fee issue relating to urban sprawl concerns the true cost of development. In the past, governments at all levels subsidized development through public construction and ignored the fact that all taxpayers supported growth. Resource scarcity in the public sector heightens the awareness that two costs are associated with development: the private costs for those who occupy new homes and buildings and the public costs to those who pay taxes and who do not use or benefit from the development.

When public financing by user fee, the costs of supporting fringe growth are perceived to require user fees on an enormous scale. These development impact fees are an example of a benefits-received approach to financing the public facilities needed to serve new growth and development. Florida has the most rigid judicial and legislative guidelines regarding the use and implementation of impact fees. A wide variety of literature, especially in the field of planning, examines the calculation and application of impact fees, related court cases, and their effects (Bridges, 1991). Impact fees do not substitute for other sources of infrastructure financing, but they are becoming an important source of financing infrastructure necessitated by new development (Campbell and Giertz, 1990).

A related development is the passage of concurrency legislation in several states to deal with the negative effects of urban sprawl. Florida's 1985 Growth Management Act includes concurrency—no development can take place unless services such as roads, water, sewer, solid waste disposal, parks and recreation, education, and health are provided at the same time as the development. Local governments are empowered to set standards for each service and to prohibit development unless these requirements are met. Communities can agree to provide the services, or developers can provide them or post bonds to ensure that necessary infrastructure and services are provided as development takes place. Florida's Department of Community Affairs coordinates and regulates the implementation of the law. Planning and zoning regulations must be coordinated on a regional and statewide basis by the local governments. If coordination is inadequate, a moratorium can be placed by the state on local development. Washington State's Growth Management Act of 1990 seeks to ensure concurrency via provisions relating to land use and capital facilities planning, transportation planning, and subdivision plat approvals linked to open space, drainage, street, sewer, water, recreation, school, and sidewalk needs.

Concurrency, often called "pay as you grow," helps to manage growth. It has many advantages in comparison to traditional "pay later" approaches. The obstacles to passage and implementation are extensive, however. As such, concurrency demands municipal-county fiscal collaboration and can be categorized as a strategy within the local government restructuring option, which is discussed next.

RESTRUCTURING THE SYSTEM OF LOCAL GOVERNMENT

The greatest likelihood for dramatic change in the local fiscal situation may lie in restructuring local government. Cigler (1993b) found three approaches that received close attention in the last decade and which receive cyclical attention: (1) the alteration of relationships between and among jurisdictions and their revenue bases within a region by creating special districts; (2) tax-base sharing among jurisdictions; and (3) transferal of powers among governments (e.g., city-county consolidations, state assumption of poverty-related responsibilities from counties, interlocal agreements, and some types of privatization) (Rivlin, 1992). Chapter 8 of this book discusses the implications of local government boundary adjustments on fiscal health. Short of restructuring, there are numerous ways that local governments cooperate on a less formal basis. Research has shown significant difficulties in organizing for collaborative relationships, however (Cigler, 1999).

PUBLIC AUTHORITIES AND SPECIAL DISTRICTS

Public authorities are the fastest growing type of government and account for approximately one-third of local government financing in the United States (Perlman 1993). Environmental Protection Agency (EPA) regulations for solid waste management, water and sewer systems, and other problems of a regional nature are increasingly handled through the creation of public authorities. Many states, for example, have formed solid waste management districts. In 1990, Indiana gave its 92 counties the option of forming multicounty districts or establishing themselves as a single-county district. Sixty-two solid waste management districts were formed: 10 were multicounty (with 40 counties) and the other 52 counties formed single-county districts. DeBoer (1992) found that smaller counties were somewhat more likely to join multicounty districts than were larger counties. The districts are new units of government with the responsibility of developing 20-year solid waste management plans to achieve waste reductions. The districts can contract for collection, recycling, and disposal facilities, as well as raise revenues via assessment of fees or property taxes.

A growing literature argues the advantages and disadvantages of public authorities (Mitchell, 1992; Axelrod, 1992). However, systematic data on authorities in general or aspects of financing are relatively sparse (Currie, Honadle, and DeBoer, 1999). Public authorities can be created by several local governments or counties, and they often operate with voter approval. They receive the power to raise revenues for both capital and operating purposes through the assessment of fees or taxes or the issuance of bonds, although many do not have taxing authority. They may also receive interest income and can apply for grants. In effect, the creation of multicounty regional authorities is a revenue diversification strategy used by cities to transfer responsibilities to the county level. Rather than directly providing the new service, however, the counties create public authorities, with county responsibility ending after appointment of the board of commissioners. There is a renewed interest in school district consolidations, especially in the Midwest.

TAX-BASE SHARING

This strategy offers a possible solution to the imbalance between public service needs and financial resources in older communities. Under such systems, a portion of all new development fees (usually limited to nonresidential development) are paid into a regional pool and redistributed by a population formula. In that way, a portion of new growth on the urban fringe is shared by the communities abandoned in the process of fueling sprawling growth. Tax-base sharing not only can reduce the incentives that drive urban sprawl but also can support the channeling of additional resources to older communities as they seek to redevelop their abandoned space. In addition, tax-base sharing can promote more orderly growth in developing jurisdictions by adding service-provision resources from the shared pool.

Jurisdictions throughout the seven-county Minneapolis–St. Paul area have been sharing the region's commercial/industrial base since 1971 via the Minnesota Fiscal Disparities Program, which provides for a regionwide pooling of 40 percent of all commercial and industrial tax base growth. The regional pool is distributed annually to the local jurisdictions based on a formula that uses the jurisdiction's population and the market value of taxable real property as variables. In 1991, metropolitan area communities shared nearly 31 percent of the region's commercial and industrial base. The program has significantly reduced tax base disparities. Sam Staley (1990) summarized the literature on tax-base sharing and completed research on several Ohio counties. A more recent review was published by Pammer and Dustin (1993), who report on cases of voluntary tax sharing in Ohio. The literature on the topic overall, however, is sparse on empirical analysis and is primarily theoretical.

Case studies by Sokolow (1993) in three counties in California's most productive and diverse agricultural area provide insight on still another type of tax-base sharing. His research demonstrates that California's tax limitation movement and the state's fiscal, programmatic, and boundary rules all constrain county finances. However, they also provide intergovernmental opportunities that enhance county finances. Specifically, the counties successfully initiated intergovernmental agreements in which affluent municipalities agreed to share their revenues with the counties. Sokolow found that county governments initiated the efforts to gain a share of municipal revenues from the reluctant municipalities. The negotiating tool possessed by the counties was the ability to thwart municipal growth plans, especially blocking city annexations. In return for some portion of municipal revenues, the cities received county support for growth actions. As Sokolow points out, state constraints on counties are ever-present, but they also can be used to empower counties in their search for alternative revenues.

Thomas and Boonyapratuang's (1993) study of 14 Texas counties demonstrates that, operating within the broad constraints set by a state, county residents shape their own patterns of governance by working within a network of government types and numbers within their region. Often, the county is not a central player, leading the authors to caution that the much-discussed prospect of reshaping of county government to emerge as a new form of metropolitan government (e.g., Fosler, 1991) is buttressed by little empirical evidence.

The structural and financial reshaping of counties to be leaders in metropolitan governance is unlikely, given the requirements of amended state constitutions and statutes needing local approval. However, counties may emerge as leaders in regional governance for rural areas (Koven and Hadwiger, 1992). There has been a substantial increase in rural county use of functional service consolidations, especially in the public safety and solid waste management areas (Cigler, 1994).

Municipalities and counties can participate in intergovernmental service contracts; joint service agreements for planning, financing, or delivering a service; and intergovernmental service transfers (i.e., the transfer of service responsibility from one government to another), although the last option is not widely authorized. Intergovernmental service contracts and joint service agreements, however, are widely used. City-county consolidations and mergers are used less frequently but are experiencing a small rise in popularity.

Privatization of public facilities is an alternative to public ownership. The private sector can provide services under contract or franchise by the government, or, in some cases, the private investor owns a specific public works facility through purchasing certificates of participation or equipment trust certificates. The most commonly used type of privatization is the contracting-out of service delivery.

TRENDS INTERACTING WITH REVENUE DIVERSIFICATION

This chapter has focused on revenue diversification options for local governments. Municipal officials in the twenty-first century will continue to work with states, counties, and each other to find alternative revenue sources. A number of events, trends, and processes—often with contradictory effects—will interact with revenue diversification efforts to affect local revenues. As Cigler (1996) has explained, these overlapping factors include:

1. New budgeting processes that incorporate the strategic planning process with the budgeting process as well as other productivity improvements that enable some cost savings.

2. Expenditure reduction efforts of all types.

3. Efforts to persuade states and the national government to provide funding for mandated programs at a time of rising service demand.

4. Court decisions that have required state assumption of costs for some mandated programs. Court decisions on school financing affect other types of local jurisdictions as all compete within a metropolitan area for the same tax base.

5. Declining interest rates due to a slow-growth national economy.

6. Demands for new, often costly, programs. Such demands are often driven by demographic changes, such as the

aging of the U.S. population, which results in the need for increased health care and hospitals, transportation, recreation, and so forth, as discussed in Chapter 3.

7. Outcomes of capital budget decisions.

8. The use of alternative service delivery (ASD) systems (e.g., functional consolidation of services, contracting-out, and so on) by all types of governments within a region.

9. The potential for a new tax limitation movement, driven by intergenerational conflict over service levels and taxation (Button and Rosenbaum, 1990).

CONCLUSIONS

In the early years of the twenty-first century, local governments are again experiencing fiscal woes, largely driven by a national recession. They, however, can turn to a wide variety of revenue enhancement, expenditure reduction, and program and administrative innovations to achieve cost efficiencies. And revenue flexibility does not have to be achieved through additional revenues. There are numerous microlevel fiscal processes that are important to a local government's general fiscal health, including purchasing, contracting and other ASD techniques, analytical techniques, and forecasting. States have broadened local investment opportunities. Financing innovations include targeting state revolving funds and bond banks to finance infrastructure (e.g., for water and sewers). A group of local governments can diminish differences among their credit ratings by issuing bonds in a pool. Alternative dispute resolution techniques can yield financial savings by lowering the costs of resolving conflicts.

When looking for ways to raise additional revenues, local governments must identify which revenue sources are underutilized and which are overutilized. Taxpayers' reactions to property taxes suggest that they are overutilized as revenue sources. However, other revenue sources may be underutilized. A useful tool in finding the underutilization or overutilization balance is revenue capacity–effort analysis, a methodology developed by the U.S. Advisory Commission on Intergovernmental Relations and refined by Ronald John Hy et al. (1992).

Local revenue systems are undergoing fundamental change. The outcomes are less influenced by national and state financial aid programs and more directly related to the economic base, political leadership, and management capacity of local governments. It is arguable, moreover, that, in the absence of an educational effort focused on taxpayers, state and local officials will continue to have difficulty devising and implementing revenue options that adequately provide necessary services in equitable ways.

A wide array of ASD options are available, but their use necessitates appropriate techniques of analysis. Chapter 5 focuses on several ASD options that can be used to reduce expenditures and increase revenues. Chapters 6 and 7 explore the use of several tools for analyzing revenue options. Chapter 8 examines structural options in depth. Chapter 9 presents a comprehensive set of strategies for communities to consider in developing their plan for being fiscally viable.

REFERENCES

Aronson, R. (1985). *Public Finance*. New York: McGraw-Hill.

Axelrod, D. (1992). *Shadow Government: The Hidden World of Public Authorities and How They Control over $1 Trillion of Your Money*. New York: John Wiley & Sons.

Bartik, T. J. (1991). *Who Benefits from State and Local Economic Development Policies?* Kalamazoo, MI: W.E. Upjohn Institute.

Bahl, R., and Duncombe, W. (1993). State and local debt burdens in the 1980s: A study in contrast. *Public Administration Review 53* (January/February), 31–40.

Bland, R. L. (1989). *A Revenue Guide for Local Government.* Washington, DC: International City/County Management Association.

Bowman, J. H., MacManus, S. A., and Mikesell, J. I. (1992). Mobilizing resources for public services: Financing urban governments. *Journal of Urban Affairs 14* (Index Issue), 311–335.

Bridges, S. V. (1991). A local government perspective on financing infrastructure. *Journal of Planning Literature 6* (November), 202–209.

Button, J., and Rosenbaum, W. (1990). Gray power, gray peril, or gray myth? The political impact of the aging in local sunbelt politics. *Social Science Quarterly 71*, 25–38.

Campbell, H. S., Jr. and Giertz, J. F. (1990). Impact fees for developing infrastructure. *Policy Forum 3* (1), 1–4.

Chang, S. Y. (1987). *A Study of the Basic Criteria and Standards for Internal Service Funds.* Lubbock, TX: Texas Tech University.

Chang, S. Y., and Freeman, R. J. (1991). Internal service funds: The neglected stepchild's neglected stepchild. *Government Accountants Journal 40* (Fall), 22–30.

Cigler, B. A. (1999). Pre-conditions for the emergence of multicommunity collaborative organizations, *Policy Studies Review, 16* (1), 86–102.

———. (1998). Emerging trends in state-local relations. In Russell L. Hanson (ed.), *Governing Partners: State-Local Relations in the U.S.* Boulder, CO: Westview Press, 53–74.

———. (1997). Local implementation of federal and state programs: Preemption, home rule, and federalism. In P. J. Cooper and C. A. Newland (eds.), *Handbook of Public Law and Administration*, San Francisco, CA, Jossey-Bass, 159–183.

———. (1996). Revenue diversification among American counties. In D. C. Menzel (ed.), *The American County: Frontiers of Knowledge.* Tuscaloosa, AL: University of Alabama Press, 166–183.

———. (1994).The county-state connection: A national study of associations of counties, *Public Administration Review, 54, 1* (January/ February), 3–11.

———. (1993a). Challenges facing fiscal federalism in the 1990s, *PS: Political Science & Politics, XXVI* (June), 181–186.

———. (1993b). State-local relations: A need for reinvention? *Intergovernmental Perspective, 19* (Winter), 15–18.

———. (1990). Public administration and the paradox of professionalization, *Public Administration Review, 506* (November/December), 637–653.

———. (1989). Trends affecting local administrators. In J. L. Perry (ed.), *Handbook of Public Administration.* San Francisco, CA: Sage Publications, 40–53.

Coe, C. K., and O'Sullivan, E. (1993). Accounting for hidden costs: A national study of internal service funds and other indirect costing methods in municipal government. *Public Administration Review 53* (1), 59–63.

Currie, E. M., Honadle, B. W., and DeBoer, L. P. (1999). Exploring the growth of special district governments: Results of a Minnesota survey, *Hamline Journal of Public Law and Policy, 21* (Fall), 67–93.

DeBoer, L. (1992). Indiana solid waste management districts. In P. F. Korsching, T. O. Borich, and J. Stewart (eds.), *Multicommunity Collaboration: An Evolving Rural Revitalization Strategy* 161–165. Ames, IA: North Central Regional Center for Rural Development, Iowa State University.

Downing, P. (1992). The revenue potential of user charges in municipal government. *Public Finance Quarterly 20* (October), 512–527.

Fosler, R. S. (1991). The suburban county: Governing mainstream diversity. *Intergovernmental Perspective, 17* (Winter), 33–37.

Gosling, J. J. (1992). *Budgetary Politics in American Governments.* New York: Longman.

Hodge, G. A. (2000). *Privatization: An International Review of Performance.* Boulder, CO: Westview Press.

Honadle, B. W. (2001). Theoretical and practical issues of local government capacity in an era of devolution, *Journal of Regional Analysis & Policy, 31* (1), 77–90

Hy, R. J., Boland, C., Hopper, R., and Simes, R. (1992). Measuring revenue capacity and effort of county governments: A case study of Arkansas. *Public Administration Review, 53* (May/June), 220–227.

Knapp, J. L., and Fox, T. J. (1992). *Special Analysis of City and County Taxes.* Charlottesville, VA: Center for Public Service, University of Virginia.

Koven, S. G., and Hadwiger, D. F. (1992). Consolidation of rural service delivery. *Public Productivity and Management Review, 15* (Fall), 315–328.

Ladd, H. F. (1992). Mimicking of local tax burdens among neighboring counties. *Public Finance Quarterly, 20* (October), 250–267.

Leonard, H. B. (1986). *Checks Unbalanced: The Quiet Side of Public Spending.* New York: Basic Books.

Liner, C. D. (1992). Alternative revenue sources for local governments. *Popular Government, 57* (Winter), 22–29.

Mields, H., Jr. (1993). The property tax: Local revenue mainstay. *Intergovernmental Perspective, 19* (Summer), 16–18.

Mikesell, J. L. (1995). *Fiscal Administration: Analysis and Applications for the Public Sector.* Belmont, CA: Wadsworth.

Mitchell, J. (1992). *Public Authorities and Public Policy: The Business of Government.* New York: Praeger.

Miller, D. Y. (2002). *The Regional Governing of Metropolitan America.* Boulder, CO: Westview Press.

Musgrave, R. A., and Musgrave, P. B. (1984). *Public Finance in Theory and Practice,* 4th ed. New York: McGraw-Hill.

Netzer, D. (1992). Differences in reliance on user charges by American state and local governments. *Public Finance Quarterly, 20* (October), 499–511.

Pammer, W. J., Jr., and Dustin, J. L. (1993). The process of fostering economic development through a county tax-sharing plan. *State and Local Government Review 25* (Winter), 57–71.

Perlman, E. (1993). Secretive governing. *City and State, March 1.*

Rivlin, A. M. (1992). *Reviving the American Dream: The Economy, the States, and the Federal Government.* Washington, DC: Brookings Institution Press.

Rourk, R. W. (1993). Assessment innovation in Orange County, Florida. *Intergovernmental Perspective, 19* (Summer), 26–28.

Savas, E. S. (2000). *Privatization and Public-Private Partnerships.* Chatham, NJ: Chatham House Publishers.

Shannon, J. (1990). The deregulation of the American federal system: 1790–1989. In T. R. Swartz and J. E. Peck (eds.), *The Changing Face of Fiscal Federalism.* Armonk, NY: M. E. Sharpe, Inc., 17–34.

Sokolow, A. D. (1993). State rules and the county-city arena: Competition for land and taxes in California's central valley. *Publius: The Journal of Federalism, 23* (Winter), 53–69.

Staley, S. (1990). Tax Base Sharing and Interjurisdictional Competition: Potential and Prospects for the 1990s. Paper presented at the Twentieth Annual Meeting of the Urban Affairs Association, Charlotte, North Carolina, April 18–21.

Thomas, J. P. (1991). Financing county government: An overview. *Intergovernmental Perspective 17* (Winter), 10–13.

Thomas, R. D., and Boonyapratuang, S. (1993). Local governmental reform and territorial democracy: The case of Florida. *Publius: The Journal of Federalism, 11* (Winter), 49–63.

Todd, B. (1991). Counties in the federal system: The state connection. *Intergovernmental Perspective, 17* (Winter), 21–25.

Ukeles, J. D. (1982). *Doing More with Less: Turning Public Management Around.* New York: Amacom.

U. S. Advisory Commission on Intergovernmental Relations. (1989). *Local Revenue Diversification: Local Sales Taxes.* Washington, DC: USACIR.

FIVE
Alternative Service Delivery Options

There are many strategies for increasing revenue generation, such as charging user fees and impacts fees, searching for new grants or economic development, raising taxes or imposing new taxes, annexing additional land, and so forth. Two other broad categories for affecting a local government's fiscal situation are program and administrative innovations to facilitate more effective and efficient service delivery and more explicit expenditure reduction strategies. Program and administrative innovations include new methods of fiscal management, such as those presented in this book, but they also include the gamut of personnel management, capital improvement programs, budgeting systems, computerized management information systems, and other strategies. Expenditure reduction strategies include increased program efficiency, the use of circuit riders or shared personnel, cutback management strategies, volunteerism, contracting, joint provision of services with other governments, private-public cooperation, and other alternative ways to deliver services.

Small governments, especially rural governments, tend to exhibit relatively low levels of activity for all but the most traditional alternatives. This is likely caused by weak management capacity. Rural governments have evolved alternative strategies for managing their finances in recognition of their different capacities and resources (Sokolow and Honadle, 1984).

Honadle's early review of research on rural areas and smaller jurisdictions (1983) offers a useful framework for understanding not only rural and small jurisdiction service delivery, but also all types of local governments. She pointed out place-specific obstacles to effective program development, service delivery, and general governance. She cited geographic isolation, low population density, mobility disadvantages, scarcity of fiscal resources, lack of expertise and human resources, personal familiarity, resistance to innovation, and a lack of ancillary services as major obstacles uncovered by researchers in their largely descriptive and traditional case study research efforts. Not all of the eight characteristics are exclusive to rural governance (e.g., scarcity of fiscal resources), but many are unique to rural areas, such as geographic isolation and low population density, and some others (e.g., scarcity of fiscal resources and lack of expertise) may have unusually negative impacts on rural areas. More recent research has confirmed the obstacles cited for small and rural governments. It has also helped to uncover the reasons for low levels of the use of enhanced revenue generation mechanisms, innovative program and administrative innovations, and a gamut of expenditure reduction tools (Cigler, 1998, 1993).

This chapter discusses an important type of expenditure reduction strategy, the use of alternative service delivery (ASD) options to reduce expenditures and achieve efficiency in the delivery of services. ASD tools were selected as a focus because of their variety and potential for achieving expenditure reduction (Honadle, 1984). Included in the chapter is a set of guidelines to follow when assessing the local government's ASD options, which were developed from a project funded by the Center for Rural Pennsylvania, a legislative agency. Written requests for materials on intergovernmental agreements and privatization options were requested from state community assistance agencies and municipal associations in the 50 states between May and September 2000. Follow-up phone calls were made to selected organizations to acquire additional information. Most helpful were the municipal associations and state community development agencies in Georgia, Michigan, New York, Arizona, Washington, and Oregon.

TYPES OF ASD OPTIONS

Popular local ASD methods include types of contracting, subsidy and fee options, and voluntary mechanisms:

Contracting Options

- Contracting out a service to the private sector
- Intergovernmental agreements to provide a service in cooperation with another local government or agency or another level of government
- Franchising out a service to the private/nonprofit sector

Subsidy/Fees Options

- Providing vouchers to local citizens to give to private service producers
- Giving a subsidy as an incentive to provide a service
- Charging user fees to achieve efficient consumption of a service

Voluntary Mechanisms

- Promoting self-help within a community
- Using volunteers to deliver all or part of a service

CRITERIA FOR EVALUATING ASD OPTIONS

Criteria such as efficiency, effectiveness, equity, and accountability are useful in evaluating the impact of the various service delivery options. Local governments need to consider these criteria when considering alternative methods of service delivery. Local governments also need to know the costs of producing the service and they need to determine methods of measuring the output of the service before considering it a viable alternative. These types of information help in monitoring the performance of the ASD methods.

The criteria for evaluating the impact of various service delivery options are defined and the contracting, subsidy or fee, and voluntary options are assessed next. The definitions used here were developed by Hirsch (1991), and the criteria were all developed and applied by Skelly (1997). The criteria developed by Hirsch and Skelly are strikingly similar to the criteria used in Chapter 4 to evaluate tax revenue options.

Efficiency—Allocative efficiency deals with optimal allocation of resources in order to maximize efficiency. Productive efficiency is further separated into technical and organizational efficiency. Technical efficiency deals with the optimal combination of inputs given quality and quantity constraints. Organizational efficiency deals with the internal organization of the service producer. Cost is used as an indicator of efficiency when it is a matter of maintaining a fixed level of quality output with a minimum level of inputs. Efficient service provision does not necessarily dovetail with low-cost service delivery. Longer hours or lower wages can reduce costs but they do not necessarily increase efficiency, for example.

Effectiveness—This criterion deals with the quality of the service delivery method from the perspective of local citizens. Do citizens believe that the quality of a service has changed as a result of a new delivery method? The private sector may be able to deliver a service at a lower cost than the public sector, but if quality is not at least maintained, then the efficiency gain is not a public benefit as rated by effectiveness. The effectiveness criterion dovetails with the adequacy criterion used in Chapter 4 to examine taxes.

Accountability—To ensure service quality and an absence of service disruptions, the service delivery entity must be accountable to its customers. To judge accountability, one must ask the following types of questions: How responsive is the delivery agent to service recipients? Is the service producer and/or provider answerable to the customer? Can dissatisfied customers effectively voice their lack of satisfaction with the service?

Equity—All social and economic segments of the municipality must be treated the same. The distribution of revenue from, or the costs of production of, an ASD method also have equity implications. This criterion dovetails with the benefits received and ability to pay logic used to evaluate taxes in Chapter 4.

The four criteria applied by Skelly (1997) to assess ASD options do not include stability; however, the elasticity or ability to grow with the economy is important both for a tax source and for an ASD option. Put simply, user fees and charges must be reexamined and sometimes increased. Intergovernmental agreements or contracts with the private sector to deliver services must be changed with changing times. Subsidies must be raised or decreased, depending on what is judged appropriate, and so forth.

Tables 5.1 through 5.4 are derived from Skelly (1997), who assessed the impact of each criterion for selected ASD options. This format can be expanded to include an even wider array of

Table 5.1   *Impact on Efficiency of Selected ASD Methods*

ASD Method	*Impact on Efficiency*
Contracting Out	Can reduce cost of delivery for some services.
Intergovernmental Agreements	Often increases efficiency, especially through economies of scale. Efficiency is decreased if extensive monitoring is required.
Franchising	Efficiency level changes depend on the specific service and whether the provider can produce at a lower cost.
User Fees	Usually results in increased efficiency since fees sometimes reflect the level of demand
Vouchers	In a competitive market, vouchers can improve efficiency, especially if a price can be assigned to the service.
Subsidy Arrangements	Should reduce the overall cost to government of service provision.
Volunteer and Self-Help	May reduce costs if services usually produced by government employees are provided and if administrative costs do not exceed these savings. There is, however, a potential for service disruption and liability costs.

ASD options, such as temporary help and regulatory or taxing authority. Here, however, the intergovernmental agreement category is scrutinized further because of its popularity. For example, a mid-1990s study of preferences for intergovernmental ASD options in Pennsylvania showed that nearly 70 percent of county officials preferred joint municipal operations, 62 percent preferred service provision through councils of governments, and 61 percent were receptive to county operation of municipal services. Less popular intergovernmental options were state delivery of particular services, preferred by 32 percent of respondents, government consolidation (31%), new tax districts (19%), and government merger (19%) (Cigler, 1997).

TABLE 5.2   *Impact on Effectiveness of Selected ASD Methods*

ASD Method	Impact on Effectiveness
Contracting Out	Can improve effectiveness but local governments must monitor the service producer/provider to ensure quality. Cost reduction may be pursued while service quality declines.
Intergovernmental Agreements	To maintain the same level of effectiveness, the expected level of service quality must be stated explicitly in the agreement among parties involved.
Franchising	Effectiveness can increase if the service provider is accountable to consumers. Standards for service quality and a monitoring system must be established.
User Fees	Service quality is not usually decreased.
Vouchers	Service quality may suffer if competition among producers is not available.
Subsidy Arrangements	The local government relinquishes control over service quality.
Volunteer and Self-Help	Service quality can increase with high-quality volunteers but volunteer quality partially depends on the commitment of the municipality to organize a volunteer program.

PERCEIVED BARRIERS TO INTERMUNICIPAL COOPERATION

Tables 5.5 and 5.6 report on the barriers to intermunicipal cooperation and ways to overcome the barriers. The suggestions were made by officials in 45 Pennsylvania local governments in face-to-face interviews in summer 2000, along with a number of state and municipal association staff (Cigler, 2002). Suggestions made dovetail closely with the existing literature on barriers to cooperation (Honadle, 1980).

The most typical agreements mentioned by the elected officials were for traditional municipal services such as law enforce-

TABLE 5.3 *Impact on Accountability of Selected ASD Methods*

ASD Method	Impact on Accountability
Contracting Out	The service producer is only indirectly accountable to customers. Municipal government must administer the contract and monitor the contract.
Intergovernmental Agreements	Maintains the same level of accountability as total local government production of a service since consumers can provide feedback to their government.
Franchising	Similar impact as contracting out. A greater level of accountability can be obtained if a non-exclusive franchise is granted since there would be more competition.
User Fees	Service providers become more accountable to consumers.
Vouchers	With competition, service providers must be responsive to customers to stay in operation.
Subsidy Arrangements	Accountability may be reduced if municipality separates itself from delivery.
Volunteer and Self-Help	Has a high potential for increasing accountability since consumers of the service also deliver it. Good management of a volunteer program increases accountability even more.

ment, emergency management, library, and fire services. Local officials claim to be most interested in receiving information about options as well as model or sample contracts. They seek such information for themselves as well as for the media, citizens, other officials, and attorneys. Table 5.5 suggests that the provision of information by those knowledgeable about ASD options is an important way to induce the consideration of such options. This capacity-building activity (Honadle, 1982) is often a major feature of state agencies and municipal and county associations that seek to promote cooperation.

TABLE 5.4   *Impact on Equity of Selected ASD Methods*

ASD Method	Impact on Equity
Contracting Out	Potential equity problems if monitoring is weak.
Intergovernmental Agreements	Equity concerns will likely be addressed since only the public sector is involved.
Franchising	No adverse effects on equity if franchise conditions require the same level of service to all segments of the population.
User Fees	Equity should improve since undercharging for services gives a subsidy to the wealthy. Varying fees based on income is difficult to implement. The fee schedule could increase with consumption.
Vouchers	This method best addresses the equity issue since those less well off can be given relatively more vouchers.
Subsidy Arrangements	Distributional effects will be specific to the service in question.
Volunteer and Self-Help	No significant distributional effects for using volunteers. Some neighborhoods may be better able to organize and implement programs than others.

The key finding from the barriers discussions, summarized in Table 5.5, is that officials most often cite a general lack of information about alternatives available as well as how to judge the alternatives when considering intermunicipal cooperation. This finding dovetails with Cigler's 1997 research on all of Pennsylvania's small counties. In that mailed questionnaire survey, the county clerk respondents perceived that a lack of information about options was the greatest barrier to cooperation. This contrasts with typical media reporting that turf protection, the inability to accept change, "politics," and other seemingly intractable variables are the greatest obstacles to the consideration and use of ASD options.

TABLE 5.5   *Perceived Barriers to Intermunicipal Cooperation and Ways to Overcome the Barriers*

Barriers to Formal Intermunicipal Cooperation	Ways to Overcome Barriers Cooperation
Transaction costs are too high at the beginning—people, money, time	Capacity-building assistance, both financial and technical; "the state should support what it promotes"; "sort out short and long costs and benefits"; sort out fixed vs. variable costs, cost shares vs. financing
Fear of loss of control	Extensive discussion among officials; exposure to success stories; data; "start easy and small"; "need clear assignment of responsibilities up-front"; need "feel good lists" to convince officials and the public
Uncertainty and complexity	Leadership; exposure to success stories; need background on range of alternatives and their suitability for different service delivery arrangements; "need help in determining whether good or service ought to be produced and/or provided by public vs. private sector"
Too many turf, power and control issues	Education about options; leadership; "don't take credit; give it"; "takes time"
Disagreement over prices to charge and allocation of cost shares when communities try to cooperate	Successful examples; model agreements; "councils of government might help"
Legal barriers to cooperation of governments of different types	Advice from state; understanding of the intergovernmental cooperation act; joint study and work session; "fire the lawyer"
Concern for sharing of risk and liability	Successful examples; model agreements; "need more information"
Too many "hidden agendas"	More interaction among officials; joint venture meetings; patience

TABLE 5.5   (continued)

Barriers to Formal Intermunicipal Cooperation	Ways to Overcome Barriers Cooperation
Difficulty in defining service areas	Professional help needed
Quantity and quality problems regarding services	Model agreements; state assistance; need help with specifications in contracts; need help in evaluating contracts; use a policy board to monitor quality
Don't know what options are available	Model agreements; computerized databases; printed materials; peer group meetings; identify leadership that can educate; "what works and what doesn't work?"
Unpleasant prior experiences	May be unresolvable; more interaction; use incremental strategies; compromise
Problems in developing agreements	Computerized databases and model agreements
Problems with administering agreements; "overwhelming administrative problems"; "process gets in the way of results wanted"	Model agreements; computerized databases; help in writing contracts and monitoring them
Disinterest of general public	Education; news media activism; workshops; public relations; "some services provided through cooperation might not otherwise be available so show citizens that"; "demonstrate how service quality and quantity are improved"; "show how specialized services might be provided"
Concern about employee job security	Targeting education strategies; "change supervisors"

Table developed from interviews with elected and appointed officials from 25 Pennsylvania communities, during field research between March and October 2000 (Cigler, 2001).

TABLE 5.6   *Perceived Barriers to Intermunicipal Agreements and Ways to Overcome Barriers*

Barriers to Formal Intermunicipal Agreements	Ways to Overcome Barriers
Money, financial, funding, rates, cost recovery	Negotiation; examine successful model agreements; more state financial and technical assistance
Too time-consuming	Negotiation; compromise; model agreements
Employee resistance	Provision of incentives; education
Deciding who should administer services, the percentage of costs paid, and what happens if the agreement is not working	Examine successful model agreements; legal action
Long-standing distrust among and between entities	Visioning, strategic processes; professional mediator
Citizen perceptions of cost, convenience, efficiency	Public meetings
Content of the agreement	Model agreements; legal advice
Deciding whether an intergovernmental agreement or contracting with the private sector is better	Examine successes and failures; know more about options and history
Concern for "effectiveness"	Measure costs and benefits; examine successes and failures elsewhere
Determining priorities, e.g., for equipment, and who "keeps the books"	Examine model agreements; examine successes and failures elsewhere
Understanding of contractual obligations	Hire good solicitors; use model agreements
Too much self-interest on part of each entity	Negotiation; get to know each other meetings
Inability to agree on salary compensation for employees	Examine successes and failures elsewhere
Distrust of county	More information needed on what counties can offer municipalities

TABLE 5.6   (continued)

Barriers to Formal Intermunicipal Agreements	Ways to Overcome Barriers
School districts own the facilities but have little interest in recreational cooperation	Obtain better data on costs and educate taxpayers
Few or no problems	"We just did it." "Education about options works." "Each town benefits if the agreement is properly developed."

Table developed from discussions with municipal association staff, state officials, and local officials involved with intergovernmental agreements—all in Pennsylvania. Discussions occurred in the offices of personnel, at association meetings, and in the home communities of local officials between March 2000 and October 2000.

Among the 45 local government participants in the Pennsylvania research in 2000, only 16 claimed to have various types of direct experience with formal intermunicipal agreements. The primary type of agreement used was within a single county, usually among two or more municipalities, with cooperation with the county, a school district, or a municipal authority less frequently used. All but two officials cited problems with the agreements. The barriers primarily involve the categories of politics, negotiations, and funding. Significantly, perceived statutory barriers received minimal mention, but other legal issues were cited, such as liability concerns. Resources, especially time needed to negotiate, financial issues, and management authority and administration were frequently mentioned. In several cases, the barriers were never resolved, yet agreements were completed.

To use ASD methods with success, several general conditions seem to apply:

- Municipal officials, citizens, the media, municipal attorneys, and others need more and better information about options for ASD, including "how to do it" information.

- A municipality should know in detail its own costs of producing a service so that cost comparisons can be made.
- If an ASD method does not work out, the municipality should retain its capacity to produce the service itself.
- Local unions need to participate in the ASD development process to ensure that their concerns are addressed.
- The public should be kept informed of ASD methods as well as the rationale for using them.
- ASD methods must be monitored.
- If privatization options are employed, there should be a sufficient number of potential bidders in the area to maintain competition and avoid a monopoly of information, compared to the local government.
- Volunteers can be used for a limited number of services, generally require training, and may entail liability.
- The use of user fees requires that service needs be measurable.
- The criteria of efficiency, effectiveness, equity, and accountability are useful for evaluating the effects of new methods on a community's services.

Table 5.6 highlights perceived barriers to intermunicipal agreements and ways to overcome those barriers. These perceptions are based on discussion groups held with local municipal association staff, state department of community and economic development staff members who work with local communities, and local elected and appointed officials who are involved with intermunicipal agreements. Although the barriers are many, so are the suggested ways to deal with them.

The field research that focused on intermunicipal relationships, especially intergovernmental agreements, included a systematic effort to review the capacity-building publications of municipal associations, such as those representing townships, boroughs, and cities, as well as manuals and handbooks developed by state agencies. Materials were received from 43 states. Information from these organizations was used to develop the following ways to assess ASD options. Publications from municipal leagues in Georgia and Michigan and state agencies in New York, Arizona, Washington, and Oregon were most helpful. Much of the material is also available on agency and association web sites in each state.

Assessing ASD Options

The success of an ASD arrangement, including an intergovernmental agreement, depends on designing, implementing, and monitoring the program successfully. The first consideration is to decide whether an ASD arrangement is the best course of action. A three-step process can accomplish this:

Step 1: Assess all ASD options.

Step 2: Analyze the service under consideration for use of an option

Step 3: Perform a cost comparison between in-house delivery and ASD.

A variety of policy, operations, finance, and personnel questions should be examined, including:

1. What is the municipality's responsibility for providing a particular service?

2.   Are there certain "essential" services that the municipality should *provide* itself?

3.   Should the municipality *be responsible* for these services?

4.   Is there a policy reason why the municipality should perform this service?

5.   Is the municipality currently providing the service in an effective manner?

6.   If not, can internal or in-house changes to improve service delivery be accomplished?

7.   Should the municipality consider using an ASD arrangement, such as an external (outside) private contractor or an intergovernmental agreement, to produce and/or provide improved service delivery?

Alternative production and/or delivery options, as well as policy options, must be considered (Kolderie, 1986; Parks and Oakerson, 1980, 1992). If a policy decision is made that the municipality should not be *responsible* for providing a certain service, then an alternative arrangement may be desirable. If the policy decision is that the municipality should be responsible for a particular service but not actually produce it, then an alternative arrangement *may* be appropriate. However, if the policy decision is that a particular service is so essential to the public health, safety, and welfare that the municipality should produce the service in-house, alternative arrangements are probably not desirable.

1. Why should a service be handled through an intergovernmental agreement or other alternative?

Increased costs and various operational issues are the major reasons why municipalities turn to ASD arrangements. It is important to conduct an analysis to evaluate whether alternatives are feasible and likely to be effective.

2. Can present costs be reduced through an ASD arrangement?

Use of an ASD arrangement stems primarily from a desire to reduce costs associated with service delivery. Escalating costs for personnel, benefits, materials, and equipment, when combined with a variety of unfunded state and national mandates, lead to the search for alternative solutions. Traditional approaches such as increases in taxes or fees and/or reductions of service levels are often unacceptable.

3. Are there considerations other than costs?

Alternative arrangements may be desirable when there is a shortage of qualified personnel to operate the service or when state and/or federal regulatory requirements make it difficult for a municipality to continue providing the service. When the service has violated state and/or federal standards for quality, resulting in fines being imposed on the municipality, or when the service does not operate efficiently or effectively, an alternative may be justified. Other considerations include a history of poor equipment maintenance, resulting in the deterioration of the municipality's capital investment; an emergency situation that reveals a significant operational deficiency in a particular service; or a service that has created a public nuisance (odors from a landfill or wastewater treatment plant, for example). When there is public dissatisfaction with a municipal service that creates adverse publicity and political pressures, an alternative arrangement may be useful. When a municipality determines, after careful analysis, that it is not feasible to continue present operations in-house, it should either redesign or reengineer the in-house operation or outsource, load shed, or use another service alternative.

4. Can a different service delivery arrangement lead to service delivery at lower costs than the current system and at a high level of effectiveness?

Savings from alternative service production and delivery are well documented. However, careful studies must be performed to determine whether cost savings are likely in a particular case. Some possible reasons for cost savings include:

- Economies of scale, with savings accrued because of larger purchases, hiring highly trained personnel, and using specialized equipment
- Better management techniques
- Better and more productive equipment
- Greater incentives to be innovative so that the arrangement is maintained
- Incentive pay structures that can boost employee performance
- More efficient use of workers
- Greater use of part-time and temporary workers
- Utilization of comparative cost information
- More work is scheduled during off-peak hours
- More careful monitoring and evaluation

5. If an alternative arrangement is used to deliver the service, will the municipality lose control of its operation?

Unless the decision is to load shed (i.e., abandon the service entirely) or to sell assets, the municipality continues to assume responsibility for the *provision* of the municipal service regardless of what entity actually delivers the service. Careful specifications in written contracts and aggressive contract monitoring and enforcement mean that the municipality has a solid degree of control over the operation of the affected service. A benefit of some alternative delivery arrangements, however, is the ability to shift some degree of accountability to another entity. The municipality still retains responsibility for ensuring that performance measures are developed and met and that the service provider is held accountable for noncompliance.

6. What options are available?

A municipality should examine carefully the various options available. For privatization, determine whether there are firms available in the local market that are capable of providing a municipal service. How many vendors are available? Competition is important because it helps to lower costs. Should a municipality look only to the private sector for service delivery or should other governmental entities, including the county or another municipality, be considered?

7. Should an in-house department of the municipality be considered? For example, could the public works department provide park maintenance services?

Popular ASD methods include various types of contracting, subsidy and fee options, and voluntary mechanisms.

CONTRACTING OPTIONS

- Contracting out a service to the private sector
- Intergovernmental agreements to provide a service in cooperation with another local government or agency or another level of government
- Franchising out a service to the private/nonprofit sector

SUBSIDY/FEES OPTIONS

- Providing vouchers to local citizens to give to private service producers

- Giving a subsidy as an incentive to provide a service
- Charging user fees to achieve efficient consumption of a service

Voluntary Mechanisms

- Promoting self-help within a community

1. Using volunteers to deliver all or part of a service

2. What legal considerations should be examined?

Carefully examine the municipal charter and local ordinances to determine if these documents allow, or more importantly, prohibit, various options. Most state laws are very permissive on intergovernmental arrangements. Various state laws and court decisions may affect the ability to privatize a service. Intergovernmental agreements are especially useful for developing a service delivery strategy to reduce unnecessary duplication of services, promote cooperation, eliminate funding inequities, and minimize interjurisdictional land use disputes.

3. Will an ASD system cause labor problems?

The effect of the privatization efforts on municipal employees requires close scrutiny. Questions arise concerning the future of the employees who presently perform the service. Will they be terminated? Will they be transferred to other municipal departments? Will the private contractor hire them or at least consider hiring them? What becomes of their employee benefits, including accrued vacation leave, sick leave, health insurance, and retirement benefits?

Strategies can be developed to address these issues and to provide for a smooth transition for employees affected by a privatization effort. Municipalities can encourage or require a contractor to hire the affected employees. Other employee displacement options include the transfer of affected employees to vacant positions in other departments; reducing staffing through attrition (eliminate certain positions as employees leave their employment); and offering early retirement and incentives that encourage the affected employees to select a one-time early retirement window option. The impact of the early retirement window on the municipality's pension funds must be considered, and any costs associated with an early retirement window should be included in the total cost estimates of the privatization effort. Obviously, the transitional options are fewer the smaller the local government.

4. Can a different service provider, such as a private provider or another government, guarantee performance and/or compliance?

There is never a guarantee that any provider will perform at the level required by the municipality. However, the municipality can and should use performance measures to monitor the ASD arrangement, with language about performance inserted into the intergovernmental or privatization agreement or contract.

5. What if the municipality is not satisfied with the agreement?

Language should be included in the agreement or contract specifying penalties for unsatisfactory work. Clauses in the agreement that specify termination conditions are useful.

Analysis of Current Operations

It is advisable to conduct an analysis of current operations for any service being considered for an alternative arrangement. Unless local officials know how well a service is performing and what a service is costing, they cannot determine whether someone else can do a better job or perform the same job at a lower cost. This can be a difficult process because many municipalities do not know the true costs of providing certain services. How much does it cost to repair a sidewalk, install a water meter, or repair a water main leak? How much does it cost to perform a building inspection on a single-family dwelling?

At a minimum, the municipality should determine the current and projected revenue and expenditure streams for the system or service, the value and condition of any capital assets, the system or service's present compliance status with state and/or national regulations, and other pertinent factors. The ability to gather complete and factual data is beneficial during all stages of the ASD decision process, including the cost comparison stage, the request-for-proposal stage (in the case of privatization options), the contract or intergovernmental agreement preparation stage, and the contract or agreement monitoring stage.

Cost Comparisons

Direct costs and overhead costs should be examined to determine the fully allocated cost, or total cost, of providing the service. To determine the true cost of in-house service delivery, the following costs must be taken into consideration.

Direct Costs—These costs include salaries, wages, employee benefits, supplies, materials, training costs, capital equipment costs, and travel costs. In addition, there are other costs that are sometimes overlooked, including interest costs, pension costs, and insurance.

Indirect Costs—These costs, also known as overhead costs, are items that benefit both the target service and another program, service, or department. An example of an indirect cost would be the salary and benefits of an employee in another department handling billing for the service delivery.

To determine the true cost of contract service delivery, these costs should be considered.

Contractor Costs—The cost that the contractor will charge for performing the privatized service may be negotiated with the contractor or opened for bids, depending on the method of contracting used. By having several companies bid on the service, market forces of competition might lower the contractor cost of privatizing the service.

Contract Administration Costs—These costs include attorney fees, staff fees for preparation, and other fees necessary to properly administer the contract.

Conversion Costs—There are costs associated with a transfer of service delivery from public providers to private providers. The particular service being privatized may have different conversion costs associated with it, such as equipment transfer and other contingency issues. Once a municipality has completed its analysis, the municipality should conduct a cost comparison between the in-house service and privatization of the service.

OUTSOURCING PRINCIPLES

Once a decision has been made to consider outsourcing, the municipality should follow a clear set of principles. The municipal charter as well as laws and guidelines for outsourcing services must be examined. There may be some stipulation that does not allow the municipality to outsource services. Amendments to the charter or operations guidelines may be necessary.

PRINCIPLES OF SUCCESSFUL CONTRACTING

Eggers (1997) provides useful guidelines for successful contracting that supplement the municipal association and state agency
materials.

1. Encourage competition.

2. Prohibit employees from having any financial or other
    interest in the contract.

3. Prohibit ex-employees from representing others such as a
    contractor before the agency. Two years prohibition after
    leaving the agency may be an appropriate period.

4. Allow bid openings and awards only in an open, public
    meeting.

5. Since most contracts are awarded based on several
    quantitative and qualitative criteria (including experience,
    rent, project concepts, rates, etc.), the municipality should
    publicize the rationale for the decision.

6. In setting standards, do not use the specification of anyone
    bidding for the contract.

7. Rely on legal counsel throughout the bidding process.

8. Once the bidding process begins, limit contact with
    contractors to the negotiation period.

9. Publicize bid awards widely and vigorously and keep a
    record of the search for contractors and the bid award.

10. Clearly define evaluation criteria and procedures and stick
    to the criteria.

Armington and Ellis (1984) also provide useful advice on the
overall outsourcing process. As public entities, municipalities are
often required to provide a competitive process when procuring

services. Guidelines are provided below for two methods of procurement.

For competitive bidding (IFB), the process should be competitive, open, and fair, with the invitation for bids publicly advertised. Bidders should submit sealed bids based on the criteria contained in the bid invitation. The municipality should open the bids publicly and evaluate each bid without discussions with the individual bidders. The contract should be awarded to the lowest responsible and responsive bidder whose bid meets the requirements and criteria contained in the bid invitation. Should the bid from the lowest responsible and responsive bidder exceed the funds budgeted for the service, the city should reserve the right to negotiate with the apparent low bidder to obtain a contract price that is within the budgeted amount.

The request for proposals (RFP) should be publicly advertised and should include conceptual program information describing the requested services in a level of detail appropriate to the project, as well as the relative importance of the evaluation factors. The city should open all proposals at the time and place designated in the RFP so as to avoid disclosure of contents to competing firms during the process of negotiations. The city should make an award to the responsible and responsive contractor whose proposal is determined to be the most advantageous to the city, taking into consideration the evaluation factors set forth in the RFP. The evaluation factors should be the basis on which the award is made.

At a minimum, the RFP should include the following considerations:

1. The amount of authority the municipality possesses over the proposed project (desired level of control) should be detailed in the RFP. This will eliminate confusion over roles and control later in the outsourcing process.

2. The municipality should consider requiring bid bonds and performance bonds. This ensures good faith by the bidding firm and eliminates many of the less capable firms from the bidding process.

3. The municipality's monitoring process should be outlined in the RFP to explain how the municipality plans to evaluate the privatized service.

Municipalities may desire to implement a process for mandatory prequalification of prospective contractors. A prequalification process allows a city to establish minimum criteria that a potential contractor must meet in order to become eligible to submit a bid or proposal for service delivery. The following guidelines are recommended should a municipality desire to pursue a prequalification process:

1. Criteria for prequalification should be reasonably related to the service to be provided and/or the quality of work to be provided. Examples of such criteria include past relevant experience with similar services, experience of personnel, and available equipment.

2. The criteria for prequalification should not be designed to eliminate all prospective providers but one.

3. The minimum criteria for prequalification should be available to any prospective provider requesting such information.

4. The process should include a method of notifying prospective providers of the minimum criteria for prequalification.

For example, the municipality's prequalification criteria should be included in the invitation to bid or request for proposal documents. Additionally, a copy of the municipality's prequalification criteria should be available at the municipal building.

CONTRACT PREPARATION AND NEGOTIATION

The contract for services should be specific. For many privatized services, some form of negotiation should take place. For example, when a municipality contracts with a private firm for operations and maintenance responsibilities, the contractual obligations generally provide the following: guaranteed performance, technical expertise and backup, training programs, community relations, reduced administrative burden on municipal staff, a stabilized budget, improved technology, elimination of employee relations problems, higher quality of operations, and additional cost savings.

To illustrate the importance of specifying precisely the service to be performed, consider this situation, which took place in a small Minnesota city. For years the city had paid a particular snowplow operator to remove snow on its streets. One year, the city decided it would be a good idea to open up the job to competitive bids. A different (low bidder) snowplow operator was hired. That particular winter had less snow than in the previous few years yet the city found itself paying more for this function than in the recent past. The reason for this unexpected outcome was that the city and the vendor did not have an agreement on performance standards. The old contractor plowed the streets only after a certain number of inches of snow had fallen and plowed more frequently at approaches to intersections than other parts of the streets. The new contractor went out and plowed all the streets whenever it snowed, regardless of the amount of snowfall. So he was billing for more work than what the city had been receiving in the past.

One of the most important elements to a successful outsourcing program is an effective system for monitoring the performance of the contractor. Municipal governments remain accountable for effective service delivery and the appropriate performance of functions. Public accountability does not evaporate simply because a service is outsourced. Contract monitoring and evaluation is an area where some local governments have failed to do their jobs. As Figure 1.2 (A Fiscal Capacity Framework) in Chapter 1 shows, it is important to evaluate current activities to guide future actions. The evaluation should assess *what* the organization is currently doing, *how much* it is doing, and *how well* it is doing it (Honadle, 1981). Municipal oversight is critically important to make sure that public funds are allocated effectively. Methods of oversight include, but are not limited to, the following: on-site inspections, both announced and unannounced; measuring goods and services against specifications; accounting and auditing procedures; performance measures; penalties; complaint monitoring; citizen satisfaction (user) surveys; field observations; and council hearings.

The ultimate key to a successful monitoring program is diligence in monitoring the service and responsiveness to ongoing needs. Again, Eggers (1997) offers useful advice for a good monitoring system.

1. Require the contractor to present periodic reports.

2. Review these reports carefully for adherence to the written contract.

3. Compare wage rates and equipment charges for materials or rentals with the contract.

4. Verify that all services, material, labor, and equipment were actually received, used, or consumed.

5. Make on-site inspections whenever possible. Report the results of these inspections, comparing accomplishment to the prescribed specifications.

6. If site inspections are not feasible (such as for a personal service contract for an attorney), keep a record of user satisfaction.

7. Follow up on every complaint.

8. Survey citizen or user satisfaction wherever possible.

CONCLUSION

Cost savings through the use of ASD tools is a valuable way to enhance revenues without raising taxes, cutting services, eliminating positions, or employing other usually undesirable measures. However, to turn to ASD options without first performing the needed analyses for ensuring success, or entering into new agreements without careful monitoring and other safeguard, could worsen the local revenue situation. Careful contract development, issuance of bids, and contract monitoring need not always be tied, either, to expensive legal assistance.

However, handshake agreements may be even more costly if ASD arrangements do not work as desired. Fortunately, officials in most local governments can turn to a variety of capacity-builders to help get started in the use of ASD options. State departments of community affairs and local municipal leagues usually can be helpful. The suggestions set forth in Table 5.5 may also be useful in achieving awareness about options as well as ways to use them. Of special note is the development of model agreements or contracts within a state that can be used by local governments to ensure sound policy and to lower legal preparation costs. Similarly, some states offer computerized databases and/or web sites to help with decision making regarding ASD. Learning from past experience is clearly an efficient way to forge better future service delivery arrangements.

DISCUSSION QUESTIONS

1. Select three services delivered by your community to citizens or families and assess the utility of using alternative delivery modes.

2. What services are delivered by your local government but are not produced by the government directly? Which services are produced and delivered by a third party such as a private company or nonprofit organization?

3. Do citizens care how a service is produced or delivered? Explain.

REFERENCES

Armington and Ellis, eds. (1984). *This Way Up: The Local Official's Handbook for Privatization and Contracting out.* Reason Foundation, Los Angeles, California.

Cigler, B. A. (2001). *Intermunicipal Cooperation in Pennsylvania*, Harrisburg, PA: Center for Rural Pennsylvania, in review.

———. (1998). Intermunicipal organizations: The untapped potential for rural Pennsylvania. The Center for Rural Pennsylvania Journal (Fall).

———. (1997). County official receptivity to intergovernmental cooperation. Middletown, PA: Pennsylvania Program to Improve State and Local Government.

———. (1993). The special problems of rural county governments. In D. Berman (ed.), *County Government in an Era of Change*, Westport, CT: Greenwood Press, 90–106.

———. (1986). Small city capacity-building and the new federalism. In J. A. Stever and L. Bender (eds.), *Administering the New Federalism.* Boulder, CO: Westview Press, 160–181.

Eggers, W. (1997). Performance-based contracting: Designing state-of-the-art contract administration and monitoring systems. Reason Foundation, Los Angeles, California.

Hirsch, W. Z. (1991). Privatizing Government Services: An Economic Analysis of Contracting Out by Local Governments. Monograph and research Series 54, Los Angeles, CA: Institute of Industrial, UCLA.

Honadle, B. W. (1984). Alternative service delivery strategies and improvement of local government productivity, *Public Productivity Review*, *8 (Winter)*, 301–313.

Honadle, B. W. (1983). *Public Administration in Rural Areas and Small Jurisdictions.* New York: Garland Publishers.

Honadle, B. W. (1982). Managing capacity-building: problems and approaches, *Journal of the Community Development Society*, *13* (2), 65–73.

Honadle, B. W. (1981). A capacity-building framework: A search for concept and purpose. *Public Administration Review*, *14*, 575–580.

Honadle, B. W. (1980). Voluntary Interlocal Cooperation: An Annotated Bibliography, Chicago: Council of Planning Librarians, Bibliography #40.

Kolderie, T. (1986). The two different concepts of privatization. *Public Administration Review*, *46* (4) *(July/August)*, 285–291.

Parks, R. B., and Oakerson, R. J. (1980). Metropolitan organization and governance. *Urban Affairs Quarterly 5 (September)*, 18–29.

Parks, R. B., and Oakerson, R. J. (1992). *Metropolitan Organization: The Allegheny County Case.* Washington, DC: USACIR.

Skelly, M. J. (1997). Alternative service delivery in Canadian municipalities. Intergovernmental Committee on Urban and Regional Research, Toronto, Ontario.

Sokolow, A. D., and Honadle, B. W. (1984). How rural local governments budget: The alternatives to executive preparation, *Public Administration Review*, *44 (Sept.–Oct.)*, 373–383.

SIX

Tools for Analyzing Local Fiscal Health

Performing a periodic analytical review of local fiscal health is a critical component in the overall practice of sound fiscal management. Information generated through the regular analysis of local government finances can serve not only to highlight a strengthening or weakening position in fiscal condition, but also to form an objective basis for critical discussions about strategic realignment of fiscal priorities. Alternatively, analysis of fiscal condition may provide confirmation of responsible stewardship of local government finances.

In this chapter three of many possible tools are discussed to analyze fiscal health, the Ten-Point Test of Fiscal Condition, the Financial Trend Monitoring System, and Fiscal Capacity Analysis.[1] We are focusing on these three, given their relative simplicity and ease of implementation. In addition, they have fairly modest data requirements for conducting the analysis of fiscal health.[2]

---

[1] For comparison of the three tools, see Beth Walter Honadle and Mary Lloyd-Jones, Analyzing Rural Local Governments' Financial Condition: An Exploratory Application of Three Tools, *Public Budgeting and Finance*, pages 69–85, Summer 1998 or Beth Walter Honadle and Mary Lloyd-Jones, University-Local Government Collaboration to Study Fiscal Health, pages 51–52, *Government Finance Review*, October 1997.

[2] When performing any type of trend analysis, the practitioner is encouraged to adjust all time series data to nominal values to control for distortions resulting from an inflationary environment. Appendix A, "Adjusting for Inflation," at the end of this chapter highlights the typical convention for making such an adjustment.

Collectively, they focus on four primary areas of fiscal health—revenues, expenditures, operating position, and debt structure. Throughout the discussion, sample data taken from Pleasant County are used to highlight the use of these tools.[3] Application of these methods to governments of varying economic and demographic composition are discussed in Chapter 7 to demonstrate how the results derived from the same methods are largely influenced by local conditions.

TOOL #1: TEN-POINT TEST OF FISCAL CONDITION

The Ten-Point Test of Fiscal Condition was developed by Kenneth W. Brown (1993). This tool portrays the fiscal condition of a local government in a set of ten simple ratios, each ratio focusing on one of four primary aspects of fiscal health–revenues, expenditures, operation position or debt structure. The beauty of Brown's tool is that it requires very few data for analysis while still being rather comprehensive in its assessment of fiscal condition. Furthermore, the Ten-Point Test method is unique in that it provides a *relative* assessment of fiscal condition. This relative assessment is obtained by utilizing the Government Finance Officer's Association (GFOA) Financial Indicators Database.[4] By comparing the financial ratios of the subject local government against those found in the database, the analyst is able to generate a relative measure of the health of their local government.

The GFOA database is comprised of financial data for city and county governments throughout the United States that have received the Certificate of Achievement for Excellence in Reporting by the GFOA for the quality of data reported.

---

[3] Although the name Pleasant County is fictitious, the data represented herein are taken from a real county government to provide "true to life" examples of actual results one might expect to obtain when applying the three tools.

[4] Updates of GFOA data for constructing the Financial Indicators Database can be ordered at http://www.estoregfoa.org.

Although this database does not represent all city and county governments nationwide, it does represent a broad spectrum of financial situations. In other words, jurisdictions with excellent reporting are not necessarily in excellent financial health. Using the GFOA Financial Indicators Database, Brown assembled the data into financial ratios broken down by population, census region, and state. Partitioning the data in this fashion allows the analyst to perform a customized comparative assessment of fiscal health by focusing attention on local governments of similar size or geographic proximity. Table 6.1 provides a detailed description of the ratios used in the Ten-Point Test.

Before the analyst can apply data from their local government to the GFOA database, one must first establish the proper benchmark for comparison. The method by which Brown accomplished this is described in the following three-step process, Preparing the GFOA Database for the Ten-Point Test:

Preparing the GFOA Database for the Ten-Point Test

1. Brown's method requires that one begin by computing each of the ten ratios for all observations of local governments in the GFOA database.

2. For each of the ten ratios computed in step 1, the data are sorted from high-to-low, or low-to-high, based on the preferred value of each ratio as indicated in Table 6.2.

    For example, a high ratio of revenues per capita (ratio 1) is generally preferred to that of a low ratio. Accordingly, the data computed in step 1 for ratio 1 were ordered from high-to-low. Ordering in this manner is performed for each of the ten ratios.

3.   Once the ratios are ordered appropriately, they are then assigned to quartiles. The middle or median observation in each ordering dictates the breakpoint of the 50th percentile. The ratios falling into the bottom 25th percentile are assigned to quartile 1. Those falling between the 25th and 50th percentile are assigned to quartile 2. The ratios falling between the 50th and 75th percentile comprise quartile 3. Finally, the remaining ratios that are greater then the 75th percentile comprise quartile 4. By doing so the most preferred value for each ratio, as indicated in Table 6.2, would always be found in quartile 4.

The three breakpoints of the 25th, 50th, and 75th percentiles between each of the quartiles establish the values of the "comparative ratios." It is against these comparative ratios that the subject local government will be evaluated. Table 6.2 depicts comparative ratios derived from the GFOA database at each of the three percentile breakpoints used when evaluating the fiscal condition of Pleasant County.

To compare the data from the GFOA database to the subject local government, the analyst then calculates 10 ratios as defined in Table 6.1 for the specific local government under study and assigns a score to each ratio as defined here:

> *Those ratios falling below the 25th percentile of all cities (or counties) receive a score* −*1, those between 25th and 50th percentiles score* 0, *between 50th and 75th score* +*1, and above 75th score* +*2.*

Once the scores for all 10 ratios have been determined, they are totaled to get an overall composite score. The overall score can also be evaluated in relative terms as shown in Table 6.3.

TABLE 6.1   *Ten-Point Test Ratios*

#	Factor	Ratio	Formula
1	Revenues	Total Revenues/Population	Total Revenue in General, Special Revenue, Debt Service, and Capital Projects Funds/Population
2	Revenues	Total General Fund Revenues from Own Sources/Total General Fund Revenues	Total Revenue less Total Intergovernmental Revenue in General Fund/Total Revenue in General Fund
3	Revenues	General Fund Sources from Other Funds/Total General Fund Sources	Total Operating Transfers into the General Fund/Total Revenue in General Fund plus transfers-in
4	Expenditures	Operating Expenditures/Total Expenditures	Total Expenditures in General, Special Revenue, Debt Service Funds/Total Expenditures in General, Special Revenue, Debt Service, and Capital Projects Funds
5	Operating Position	Total Revenues/Total Expenditures	Total Revenue in General, Special Revenue, Debt Service, and Capital Projects Funds/Total Expenditures in General, Special Revenue, Debt Service, and Capital Projects Funds
6	Operating Position	Unreserved General Fund Balance/Total General Fund Revenues	Unreserved, Designated and Undesignated Fund Balance in General Fund/Total Revenue in General Fund
7	Operating Position	Total General Fund Cash and Investments/Total General Fund Liabilities	Total Cash and Investments in General Fund/Total Assets in General Fund less Reserved and Unreserved Fund Balances
8	Debt Structure	Total General Fund Liabilities/Total General Fund Revenues	Total Assets in General Fund less Reserved and Unreserved Fund Balances/Total Revenue in General Fund
9	Debt Structure	Direct Long-Term Debt/Population	General Obligation Debt to be repaid from Property Tax Revenue/Population
10	Debt Structure	Debt Service/Total Revenues	Total Expenditures in Debt Service Fund/Total Revenue in General, Special Revenue, Debt Service, and Capital Projects funds

Source: Brown, Kenneth W., 1996 edition of the Ten-Point Test of Financial Condition, Solstice Productions, June 1996.

TABLE 6.2   *Comparative Ratios for Counties*

Ratio	Ratio #	Preferred Value	Quartile Breakpoints		
			25%	50%	75%
Total Revenues/Population	1	High	395.305	566.542	511.781
Total General Fund Revenues from Own Sources/ Total General Fund Revenues	2	High	0.768	0.865	0.877
General Fund Sources from Other Funds/Total General Fund Sources	3	Low	0.020	0.006	0.000
Operating Expenditures/ Total Expenditures	4	Low	0.975	0.945	0.900
Total Revenues/ Total Expenditures	5	High	0.963	1.011	1.079
Unreserved General Fund Balance/Total General Fund Revenues	6	High	0.156	0.332	0.393
Total General Fund Cash and Investments/Total General Fund Liabilities	7	High	0.435	1.022	2.415
Total General Fund Liabilities/ Total General Fund Revenues	8	Low	0.286	0.210	0.162
Direct Long-Term Debt/ Population	9	Low	176.106	73.946	1.992
Debt Service/ Total Revenues	10	Low	0.031	0.013	0.000

Comparison Group—Counties by Census Region and Population.
U.S. Census Midwest Region, Population Range: Below 100,000. Reproduced from Brown, Kenneth W., 1997. Edition of the *Comparative Ratios for Counties*, Solstice Productions.

APPLICATION OF THE TEN-POINT TEST TO PLEASANT COUNTY

The data for the Ten-Point Test typically are taken from financial statements maintained by the local government. Table 6.4 provides a sample of four years of data used in Pleasant County to perform the Ten-Point Test.

TABLE 6.3   *Table of Overall Ranking*

Overall Score	Evaluation of Overall Score
14	99th percentile 1% of GFOA counties scored higher
12	95th percentile 5% of GFOA counties scored higher
10	90th percentile 10% of GFOA counties scored higher
8	75th percentile 25% of GFOA counties scored higher
5	50th percentile 50% of GFOA counties scored higher
2	25th percentile 75% of GFOA counties scored higher
0	10th percentile 90% of GFOA counties scored higher
−2	5th percentile 95% of GFOA counties scored higher
−4	1st percentile 99% of GFOA counties scored higher

Source: Brown, Kenneth W., 1996 Edition of the Ten-Point Test of Financial Condition, Solstice Productions, June 1996.

Using data for Pleasant County from Table 6.4, the 10 ratios have been computed for the years 1999 through 2002 and displayed in Table 6.5.

By using the reference comparative ratios in Table 6.2, along with the subject government's ratios as shown in Table 6.5, the analyst can generate a snapshot of fiscal condition for each year. By conducting the Ten-Point Test for multiple years, the analyst combines the benefits of a relative assessment with that of a trend analysis. Such a combined analysis is depicted in Table 6.6, with each of the 10 ratios and their associated scores for multiple years. In this instance we provide an analysis of fiscal health with 131 other counties in the Midwest with populations under 100,000 as our reference point. This partition of the GFOA database was selected because it closely approximates the geographic and population size characteristics of Pleasant County.

The findings reveal that Pleasant County's fiscal condition as of 2002 was relatively sound when compared with all other counties in the GFOA database. In terms of overall score, the results

TABLE 6.4   *Pleasant County's Ten-Point Test Data*

Ratio	1999	2000	2001	2002
Population	10,398	10,473	10,558	10,69
Total revenues	$14,008,522	$15,505,706	$17,329,825	$16,740,224
Total general fund revenues—own sources	$3,229,997	$3,310,496	$3,370,009	$3,297,914
General fund sources from other funds	$6,689,684	$7,793,822	$9,482,088	$8,797,008
Total general fund sources	$9,989,681	$11,104,318	$12,852,097	$12,094,922
Operating expenditures	$11,510,163	$12,728,773	$14,686,576	$14,057,233
Total expenditures	$12,422,734	$13,945,386	$17,404,246	$17,132,584
Unreserved general fund balance	$3,275,970	$4,310,760	$4,820,446	$4,503,938
Total general fund revenues	$5,400,837	$5,513,057	$5,714,217	$6,594,155
Total general fund cash and investments	$8,331,960	$9,438,986	$10,676,984	$10,608,698
Total general fund liabilities	$996,250	$480,169	$987,649	$591,751
Direct long-term debt	$4,844,024	$933,261	$2,405,642	$2,805,856
Debt service	$563,393	$847,079	$732,205	$765,481

of this study (Table 6.6) show that Pleasant County received scores of 6, 7, 6, and 7 for the years 1999 though 2002, respectively. These overall scores imply that Pleasant County placed in the 50th to 75th percentiles during all four years. This outcome is a little better than average in terms of relative fiscal health.

A look at the individual ratio score for each of the four categories of fiscal condition—revenues, expenditures, operating

TABLE 6.5   *Pleasant County Ten-Point Test Ratios*

Ratio	Ratio #	1999	2000	2001	2002
Total Revenues/Population	1	1347.23	1480.54	1641.39	1565.24
Total General Fund Revenues from Own Sources/Total General Fund Revenues	2	0.6110	0.6005	0.5898	0.5001
General fund Sources from Other Funds/Total General Fund Sources	3	0.6697	0.7019	0.7378	0.7273
Operating Expenditures/ Total Expenditures	4	0.9265	0.9128	0.8439	0.825
Total Revenues/ Total Expenditures	5	1.128	1.112	0.995	0.977
Unreserved General Fund Balance/Total General Fund Revenues	6	0.6065	0.7819	0.8436	0.6830
Total General Fund Cash and Investments/Total General Fund Liabilities	7	8.36	19.66	10.81	17.93
Total General Fund Liabilities/Total General Fund Revenues	8	0.1845	0.0871	0.1728	0.0898
Direct Long-Term Debt/ Population	9	465.86	89.11	227.85	262.35
Debt Service/ Total Revenues	10	0.0402	0.0546	0.0423	0.0457

TABLE 6.6 *Sample Ten-Point Test Results—Summary And Interpretation For Pleasant County*

Ratio	Ratio #	1999		2000		2001		2002	
		Ratio	Score	Ratio	Score	Ratio	Score	Ratio	Score
Total Revenues/Population	1	1347.23	2	1480.54	2	1641.39	2	1565.24	2
Total General Fund Revenues from Own Sources/Total General Fund Revenues	2	0.6110	-1	0.6005	-1	0.5898	-1	0.5001	-1
General fund Sources from Other Funds/Total General Fund Sources	3	0.6697	-1	0.7019	-1	0.7378	-1	0.7273	-1
Operating Expenditures/Total Expenditures	4	0.9265	1	0.9128	1	0.8439	2	0.825	2
Total Revenues/Total Expenditures	5	1.128	2	1.112	2	0.995	0	0.977	0

6	Unreserved General Fund Balance/Total General Fund Revenues	0.6065	2	0.7819	2	0.8436	2	0.6830	2
7	Total General Fund Cash and Investments/Total General Fund Liabilities	8.36	2	19.66	2	10.81	2	17.93	2
8	Total General Fund Liabilities/Total General Fund Revenues	0.1845	0	0.0871	1	0.1728	1	0.0898	1
9	Direct Long-Term Debt/Population	465.86	-1	89.11	0	227.85	0	262.35	0
10	Debt Service/Total Revenues	0.0402	0	0.0546	-1	0.0423	0	0.0457	0
	Overall Score:		6		7		6		7
	Percentile Rank:		50th–75th		50th–75th		50th–75th		50th–75th

Brown, Kenneth W., 1996 Edition of the *Ten-Point Test of Financial Condition*, Solstice Publications, June 1996.

position, and debt structure—provides a more focused description of fiscal condition. When doing so, we see that the category of operating position demonstrated the best overall performance during the four studied years. Ratios 6 and 7 received $^+2$ from 1999 to 2002 and indicate that the county's liquidity position is quite strong. Furthermore, ratio 4 also received high marks, particularly in 2001 and 2002. This result suggests that Pleasant County is maintaining its infrastructure adequately.

Ratios 8, 9, and 10 describe the fiscal condition of the county as it relates to total bonded indebtedness and the ability of the county to service its debt burden. Here we find, relatively speaking, that the debt level on a per capita basis is a little high. Additionally, the ability of the county to meet debt service requirements when due may be in question as a result of this relatively high level of debt. The final category of fiscal condition pertains to revenues. Ratio 1 did receive a $^+2$ for all four studied years, which by itself is a sign of strength for Pleasant County. However, such a high score must be evaluated in the context of the other ratios. Ratios 2 and 3 indicate that the *composition* is largely from sources *outside* the county. The implication of a relatively high level of outside revenue sources is that the county may be overly dependent on external government organizations for revenues. A potential problem arises if state or national policy changes so that funding is reduced or eliminated. Given the highly political nature of such funding sources, it is always advisable to be cautious of the possible short-term nature of outside funding.

In summary, the Ten-Point Test results indicate that the overall fiscal condition of Pleasant County appears to be reasonably sound. Some particular signs of strength would be liquidity and infrastructure expenditures. Areas to watch would be debt levels and reliance on outside revenue sources. In general, the Ten-Point Test is a good way to perform a quick and easy check-up on a yearly basis. Requiring only 13 data points to compute ten ratios, its simplicity is its virtue, but it is also somewhat short on detail. The lack of granularity found in the Ten-Point Test is addressed through application of the following two tools.

Tool #2: Fiscal Capacity Analysis

The Fiscal Capacity Analysis tool was developed by Theodore Alter and colleagues at Penn State University (Alter, McLaughlin, and Melniker). Fiscal Capacity Analysis uses five-year trends to forecast revenues and expenditures. Unlike the Ten-Point Test, the Fiscal Capacity Analysis tool does not examine the fiscal condition as a snapshot in time. Instead, it benefits from a long data history to develop trends of revenue and expenditure patterns. First, the analyst prepares a history of revenues and expenditures. This step involves separating revenues and expenditures into categories small enough to make it possible to identify factors that affect a particular category. We have used Alter's recommended guideline of 5 percent of total revenues. By limiting the categories to be graphed to only those that are 5 percent or less of total revenues, we are able to clearly see changes in revenue and expenditure patterns. The 5 percent cutoff is an arbitrary number; one could use a cutoff of 10 percent or 15 percent. However, a higher cutoff level would likely hide revenue and expenditure patterns, which become clear at a level of 5 percent. Therefore, we follow Alter's recommendation and use 5 percent of total revenues.

The individual categories are then plotted over time to find fiscal trends. For the trends to make sense, administrative changes and one-time events must be identified, such as changes in tax rates or assessment ratios, changes in number of employees, adding or eliminating a service, and so forth. These discretionary changes can distort a trend, making it useless for prediction purposes.

When possible, it is preferable to adjust historical data to reflect a discretionary change. For instance, if the property tax rate increased, one should recalculate what the tax revenue would have been if the new rate had been in effect for the whole history. Then the trend would show revenue based on the growth of the tax base, not on administrative changes. While failure to account for such changes directly in the data does not preclude one from proceeding with the analysis, it does however place a greater burden on the analyst when interpreting historical trends.

The data used to calculate these trends for Pleasant County came from the local government budget for the years 1998 through 2002. Again, only the categories that met the cutoff of less than 5 percent of total revenues were included in this analysis. Table 6.7 illustrates the data used in the Fiscal Capacity Analysis. It is followed by a number of examples in which the same data were used to plot trends.

The Fiscal Capacity Analysis tool is especially useful for projecting trends in particular areas and thereby helpful in efforts directed toward controlling expenditures. For example, the governing board may know that public safety costs are escalating. However, this is such a broad category that it is desirable to disaggregate the data into smaller expenditure categories to pinpoint the source of the problem. Likewise, local officials may be concerned with a decline in intergovernmental aid. Conducting the Fiscal Capacity Analysis will help them see exactly what national or state financial aid programs are driving an overall decline.

TABLE 6.7 *Pleasant County's Fiscal Capacity Analysis Data*

Nominal figures

		1998	1999	2000	2001	2002
5% of Total Revenues		$895,077	$1,412,647	$1,593,601	$1,302,520	$1,320,644
Revenues	Special Assessments	$151,707	$434,630	$678,519	$713,326	$474,189
	Licenses & Permits	$212,825	$261,669	$282,317	$367,866	$429,210
	Federal Grants:					
	Narcotics Control	$28,299	$30,000	$30,000	$30,000	$25,000
	Highways	$15,825	n/a	$2,341	$722,543	$6,378
	All Other	$199,066	$172,504	$82,462	$73,950	$119,923
	State Grants:					
	Homestead Credit	$44,445	$46,557	$48,843	$50,622	$52,303
	Machinery Aid					
	Disparity Reduction	$6,671	$5,177	$7,007	$6,942	$6,942
	Highways				$1,054,017	
	Other	$493,152	$644,841	$623,947	$933,028	$851,650
	Local Grants	$44,185	$36,303	$54,738	n/a	$21,162

Table 6.7   (continued)

Fines	$243,804	$699,860	$746,133	$681,739	$304,624
Interest Earnings	$434,708	$431,492	$599,253	$797,289	$782,664
All Other Revenue	$1,157,463		$1,210,438		$1,263,107
Borrowing:					
Bonds Issued				$490,000	
Other Long-Term Debt		$184,965		$419,915	$39,100
Expenditures					
General Government					
Capital Outlay	$81,060	$3,052	$72,938	$490,667	$154,640
Public Safety:					
Sheriff			$1,305,557		
Corrections	$734,789	$868,979	$1,318,383	$1,373,052	$1,477,569
Other	$134,248	$158,620	$180,978	$231,291	$293,783
Streets & Highways:					
Administration	$292,719	$255,065	$358,950	$434,768	$499,725

Operation & Maintenance		$1,283,024	$1,359,361	$1,114,488	$1,219,877
Sanitation	$272,322	$667,356	$567,646	$461,989	$357,267
Health	$914,909	$850,794	$951,834	$1,445,393	$1,423,458
Library	$130,284	$140,039	$148,933	$177,309	$177,750
Parks & Rec.	$95,117	$98,468	$97,685	$136,740	$163,311
Conservation of Natural Resources	$201,725	$189,330	$184,404	$268,800	$358,608
Economic Development	$101,966	$148,058	$223,858	$283,924	$532,836
Miscellaneous Expenditures		$1,310,291	$1,334,117		$1,019,778
Interest & Fiscal Charges	$848,174	$849,131	$1,229,893	$1,228,501	$927,541
Principal (Debt Service)		$590,000	$635,000	$770,000	
Other Long-term Debt		$17,049	$198,974	$15,000	$15,000

A blank space in this table does not necessarily mean that the county does not have this revenue or expenditure. Rather, a blank space means that this revenue/expenditure was not less than 5% of total.

Sample results of the fiscal capacity analysis—Pleasant County.

Revenues

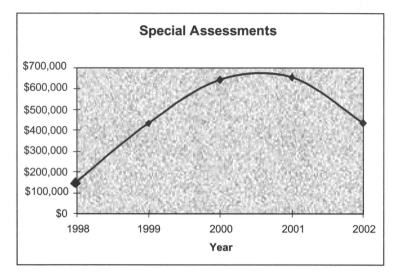

FIGURE 6.1 *Special Assessments, 1998–2002. A Special Assessment is defined as a levy against a property to offset the costs of a specific improvement to the property. The amount assessed is based on how much the individual property benefits from the improvement. Any penalties and interest paid on the assessment are included in this graph. The variation in this graph can be explained by changes in Pleasant County's solid waste fee that constitutes approximately 80% of special assessments. The County originally charged $20 in 1998 for this fee and then increased it to $40 in 2000 & 2001. It was later reduced to $25 in 2002*

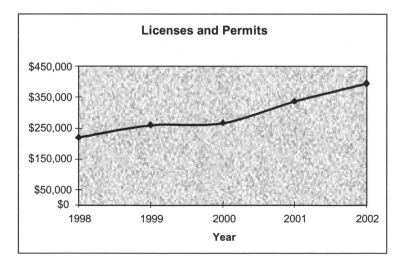

FIGURE 6.2 *Licenses and Permits, 1998–2002. Licenses and Permits as a revenue category showed a steady increase over the time period as the Pleasant County board increased the price of licenses and added new permit charges to cover county expenses*

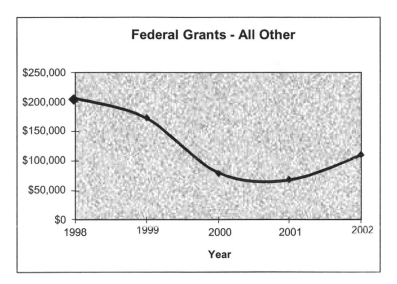

FIGURE 6.3   *Federal Grants–All Other, 1998–2002. This category includes all federal grants that are not individually categorized in the State Auditor's report. This excludes federal grants for highways, human services and narcotics control.*

Expenditures

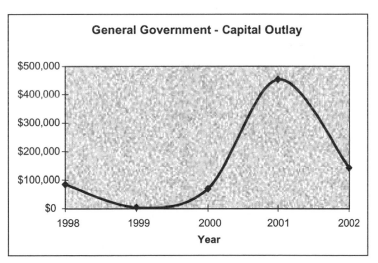

FIGURE 6.4   *General Government–Capital Outlay, 1998–2002. General government-capital outlay includes expenditures for the purchase or construction of buildings, permanent improvements, equipment, machinery and land for the day-to-day operation of the government. This category shows a large one-time jump in 2001. Investigation into this event is recommended.*

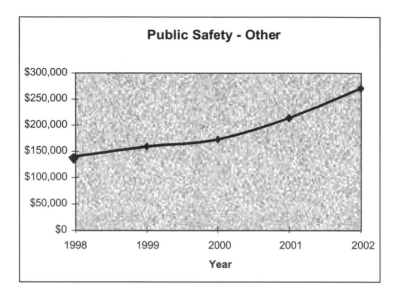

FIGURE 6.5 *Public Safety-Other, 1998–2002. This classification is comprised of expenditures on public safety excluding those on sheriff, corrections, and capital outlay. It does include such areas as civil defense. In Pleasant County other public safety expenditures increased modestly over the time period*

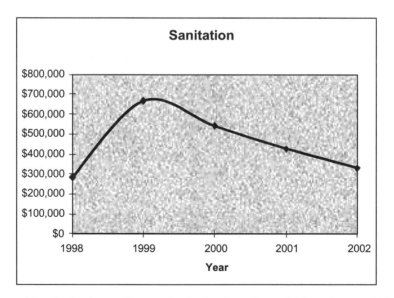

FIGURE 6.6 *Sanitation, 1998–2002. Sanitation showed a major jump in 1999. This was followed by a steady decrease over the rest of the time period. The Solid Waste Commission built a waste facility in the county that was expected to be self-sufficient. In 1999 Pleasant County was required to assist in the payment of bonds for this facility, which largely accounts for the peak in this graph in 1999*

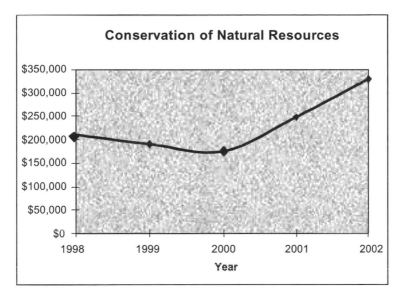

FIGURE 6.7   *Conservation of Natural Resources, 1998–2002. Conservation of natural resources, as defined by the State Auditor's Report, are activities designed to conserve and develop natural resources, including water, soil, forest and minerals.*

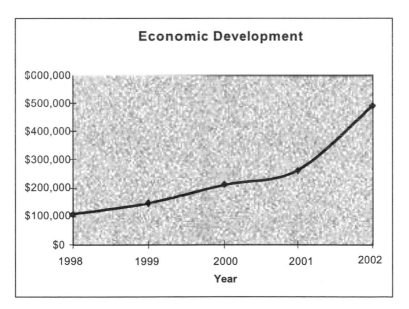

FIGURE 6.8   *Economic Development, 1998–2002. Expenditures for economic development include expenditures for providing adequate housing and for development of business. Pleasant County showed steady increase until 2002 when expenditures jumped substantially*

Tool #3: The Financial Trend Monitoring System

The International City/County Management Association (ICMA) developed a set of 36 indicators (Groves and Godsey-Valente, 1994) for evaluating the financial condition of cities and counties. These indicators are collectively known as the Financial Trend Monitoring System (FTMS). As in the Ten-Point Test, the FTMS covers such aspects as revenues, expenditures, operating position, and debt structure. The indicators are plotted over a five-year period to show "warning trends." Since much of the data cannot be found in regular financial statements, the FTMS indicators are somewhat more demanding to work with than the other two tools. Occasionally the data can be found, but often they are not presently organized in the correct format to calculate the indicators. Hence, selecting among the 36 possible indicators is a function of both data availability and relevance to the needs of local government. Accordingly, selection decisions should be made in collaboration with local government administrators.

Application of the FTMS provides rich detail of local fiscal health through its definition of 36 financial indicators and associated warning signs. While at present it is likely that the local government would not have sufficient data to plot every historical trend, calculate each financial ratio, or compute each of the 36 ICMA indicators, proactive data management can pay handsome dividends in future years. Where the local government finds it is currently lacking in financial data, officials are encouraged to be proactive in ongoing maintenance of financial records. As with the Ten-Point Test and the Fiscal Capacity Analysis tools, diligent keeping of local financial records, both historically and moving forward, allows the analyst great freedom in either selective or comprehensive application of each tool. With a more complete data repository on which to draw, the analyst will be better enabled to formulate a complete picture of the fiscal condition of the local government.

Given the hypothetical preferences of Pleasant County officials and taking into account data limitations, we analyzed 11 of the FTMS indicators for Pleasant County. Table 6.8 lists the 36 ICMA indicators followed by a sample of five years of data used in the FTMS tool for Pleasant County, presented in Table 6.9.

TABLE 6.8   *ICMA's 36 Indicators for the Financial Trend Monitoring System*

Indicator Number and Title	Formula Used to Develop the Trend
1. Revenues per Capita	Net Operating Revenues (constant dollars)/Population
2. Restricted Revenues	Restricted Operating Revenues/Net Operating Revenues
3. Intergovernmental Revenues	Intergovernmental Operating Revenues/Gross Operating Revenues
4. Elastic Tax Revenues	Elastic Operating Revenues/Net operating Revenues
5. One-Time Revenues	One-time Operating Revenues/Net Operating Revenues
6. Property Tax Revenues	Property Tax Revenues (constant dollars)
7. Uncollected Property taxes	Uncollected Property Taxes/Net Property Tax Levy
8. User Charge Coverage	Revenues from Fees and User Charges/Expenditures for Related Services
9. Revenue Shortfalls	Revenue Shortfalls/Net Operating Revenues
10. Expenditures per Capita	Net Operating Expenditures (constant dollars)/Population
11. Employees per Capita	Number of Municipal Employees/Population
12. Fixed Costs	Fixed Costs/Net Operating Expenditures
13. Fringe Benefits	Fringe Benefit Expenditures/Salaries and Wages
14. Operating Deficits	General Fund Operating Deficits/Net Operating Revenues

TABLE 6.8 (continued)

Indicator Number and Title	Formula Used to Develop the Trend
15. Enterprise Losses	Enterprise Profits or Losses (constant dollars)
16. Fund Balances	Unreserved Fund Balances/Net Operating Revenues
17. Liquidity	Cash and Short-term Investments/Current Liabilities
18. Current Liabilities	Current Liabilities/Net Operating Revenues
19. Long-Term Debt	Net Direct Bonded Long-term Debt/Assessed Valuation
20. Debt Service	Net Direct Debt Service/Net Operating Revenues
21. Overlapping Debt	Long-Term Overlapping Bonded Debt/Assessed Valuation
22. Unfunded Pension Liability	Unfunded Pension Liability/Assessed Valuation
23. Pension Assets	Pension Plan Assets/Annual Pension Benefits Paid
24. Accumulated Employee Leave	Total Days of Unused Vacation and Sick Leave/Number of Municipal Employees
25. Maintenance Effort Quantity of Assets	Expenditures for Repair and Maintenance of General Fixed Assets (constant dollars) /
26. Capital Outlay	Capital Outlay from Operating Funds/Net Operating Expenditures
27. Depreciation Expense	Depreciation Expense/Cost of Depreciable Fixed Assets
28. Population	Population
29. Median Age	Median Age of Population
30. Personal Income per Capita	Personal Income (constant dollars)/Population
31. Poverty Households or Public Assistance Recipients	Poverty Households or Pub. Assistance Recipients/Households in Thousands
32. Property Value	Change in Property Value (constant dollars)/Property Value in Prior Year (constant dollars)
33. Residential Development	Market Value of New Residential Development/Market Value of Total New Development

TABLE 6.8 (continued)

Indicator Number and Title	Formula Used to Develop the Trend
34. Vacancy Rates	Vacancy Rates
35. Employment Base	Local Unemployment Rate and/or the Number of Jobs within the Community
36. Business Activity	• Retail Sales • Number of Business Units • Gross Business Receipts • Number of Acres Devoted to Business • Market or Assessed Value of Business Property

See S. Groves and M. Valente, 1994, for further details regarding use of the 36 indicators.

TABLE 6.9 *Pleasant County's Financial Trend Monitoring System Data*

Specific Data Required	1993	1994	1995	1996	1997
Gross operating revenues	12,570,729	14,008,522	15,505,706	17,329,825	16,740,224
Net operating revenues	11,820,094	13,156,472	14,453,748	16,352,424	15,806,275
Restricted operating revenues					
Intergovernmental operating revenues	6,136,538	6,689,684	7,793,822	9,482,008	8,797,008
Elastic operating revenues					
Property tax revenues	3,141,338	3,231,357	3,195,622	3,262,843	3,208,211
Uncollected property taxes	71,650	68,640	114,874	107,166	89,703
Net property tax levy	3,212,988	3,299,997	3,310,496	3,370,009	3,297,914
Revenues from fees and user charges	512,142	639,259	678,985	654,446	6,755,968
Expenditures for related services	100,254	65,796	46,346	47,277	55,033
Net operating expenditures	10,555,960	11,510,163	12,728,773	14,686,576	14,057,233
Number of municipal employees	121	119	121	122	124

TABLE 6.9   (continued)

Specific Data Required	1993	1994	1995	1996	1997
Fixed costs					
Fringe benefits expenditures	729,172	896,222	919,143	933,524	960,770
Salaries and wages	3,678,195	3,764,737	3,889,353	4,081,813	4,259,650
General fund operating deficits					
Unreserved fund balances	5,713,001	7,079,096	9,327,503	9,830,416	9,966,690
Cash and short-term investments	6,419,154	8,331,960	9,438,986	10,676,984	10,608,698
Current liabilities					
Net direct bonded long-term debt	1,695,000	1,480,000	903,700	2,185,000	2,145,000
Certificates of participation					
Net direct debt services	588,811	563,393	847,079	732,205	765,481
Long-term overlapping bonded debt					
Unfunded pension plan liability					
Pension plan assets	260,150	264,416	270,592	274,539	283,763
Pension benefits paid					
Quantity of assets					
Capital outlay	104,462	77,468	3,900	1,604,305	1,796,354
Depreciation expense (enterprise and internal service funds)					
Population	10,363	10,398	10,473	10,558	10,695
Median age of population					
Personal income					
Poverty households					
Public assistance recipients				578	525

TABLE 6.9   (continued)

Specific Data Required	1993	1994	1995	1996	1997
Residential households	4,245	4,258	4,294	4,338	4,419
Assessed value of residential, commercial, and industrial property*	4,632,346	4,976,538	5,472,976	5,904,454	6,079,267
Gross business receipts					
Number of acres devoted to business					

* tax capacity

A blank space on this worksheet does not equate to a value of zero. Rather, a blank space indicates the county was not required to provide this information in order to plot the chosen FTMS indicators.

Sample Results from the Financial Trend Monitoring System—Pleasant County.

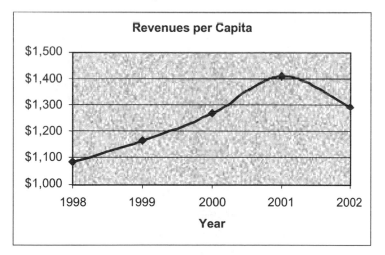

FIGURE 6.9   *Indicator #1: Revenues per Capita, 1998–2002. This indicator is calculated as: net-operating revenues in constant dollars divided by population. A decreasing level of revenues per capita would be a warning sign of deteriorating fiscal condition. With the exception of the most recent year, 2002, revenues per capita have been consistently increasing. This is a sign of fiscal strength for Pleasant County. The latest decline in 2002 may be a one-time event or the beginning of a negative tend. Continued monitoring is warranted*

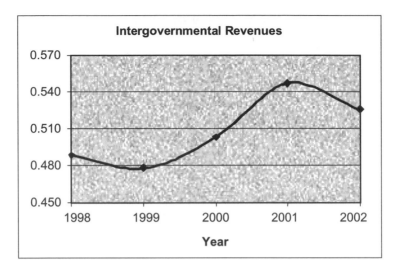

FIGURE 6.10   *Indicator #3: Intergovernmental Revenues, 1998–2002. This indicator is defined as: intergovernmental operating revenues over gross operating revenues. ICMA designates a warning sign to be an increasing level of intergovernmental revenues. The graph depicts just such a trend from the years 1999–2001. Further analysis of this indicator is warranted being that an overdependance on intergovernmental revenues may put in question the long-term the fiscal health of the local government*

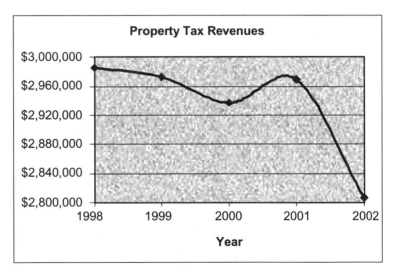

FIGURE 6.11   *Indicator #6: Property Text Revenues, 1998–2002. Indicator six is simply a graphical depiction of property tax revenues in constant dollars. A warning sign would be a declining trend. Data for this indicator suggest a fairly stable level of property tax revenues during the years 1998–2001. However, between the years 2001 and 2001 we observe a decline of more than 5%. This is of concern since property tax revenues typically comprise a large portion of local government revenues*

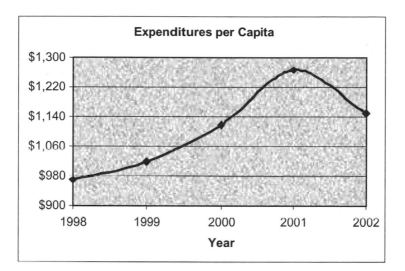

FIGURE 6.12   *Indicator #10: Expenditures per Capita, 1998–2002. Indicator #10 is defined as: net-operating expenditures in constant dollars divided by population. A warning sign for this indicator would be an increasing trend. We do observe such a trend for the years 1998–2001. An increasing level of expenditures per capita can suggest that the cost of providing services is outpacing the community's ability to pay for those services. The decline in 2002 is a welcome sign for Pleasant County*

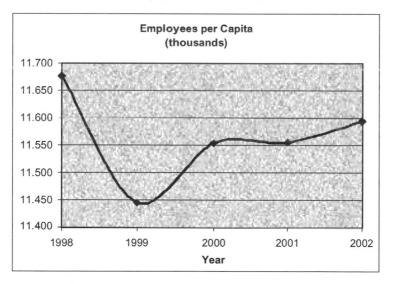

FIGURE 6.13   *Indicator #11: Municipal Employees per Capita, 1998–2002. This indicator depicts the total number of municipal employees per every thousand residents. It is an important measure since expenditures on personnel represent a significant portion of a local government's operating budget. An increasing trend might suggest that the government is becoming more labor intensive or that personnel productivity is declining. Although the graph for Pleasant County reveals an increasing trend, the change is quite small in relative terms*

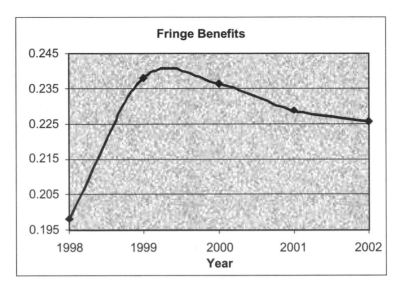

FIGURE 6.14 *Indicator #13: Fringe Benefits, 1998–2002. The fringe benefits indicator is defined as all expenditures on fringe benefits divided by total salaries and wages. A trend that is increasing would be a warning sign as outlined by the ICMA. Fringe benefit expenditures generally represent 30% of total employee compensation costs.*

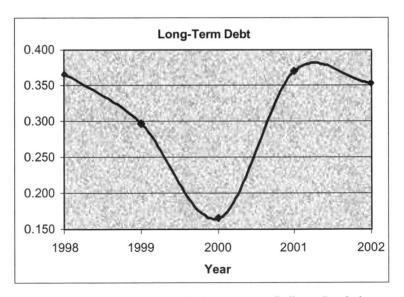

FIGURE 6.15 *Indicator #19: Long-term Debt, 1998–2002. Indicator #19 depicts net-direct bonded debt as a percentage of assessed property valuation. Assuming that the local government is relying on property taxes to repay its debt, a decline in this indicator would suggest that the ability of the local government to repay its long-term debt is diminishing. Due to the fluctuation in this graph it is difficult to discern a meaningful trend. Consequently, further analysis is recommended*

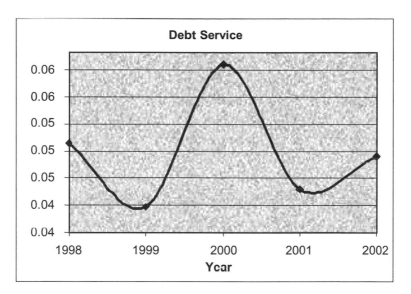

FIGURE 6.16   *Indicator #20: Debt Service, 1998–2002. Debt service is defined as: net–direct debt service as a percentage of net operating revenues. One can readily notice the inverse relationship between indicators #19 and #20 (above). Together these graphs suggest 2000 was a year where increases in debt service payments were attributable to the retirement of a large share of outstanding long–term debt. In the absence of such increased payments, indicator #20 demonstrates relative stability in debt service burden over the studied years*

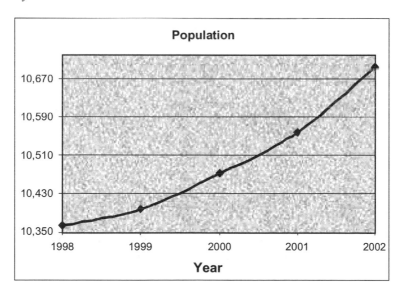

FIGURE 6.17   *Indicator #28: Population, 1998–2002. Changes in population affect the fiscal condition of a local government in many ways. These effects range from the demand for services provided by the local government to the ability of the local government to pay for such services via tax revenues. Given that a sharp population decline or increase would place significant fiscal pressure on a local government, ICMA merely notes that a rapid change in any given population level is a warning sign. As shown by the graph, the population of Pleasant County has been steadily increasing at a rate of nearly 3.2%*

CONCLUSION

Periodic application of the Ten-Point Test of Fiscal Condition, the FTMS, and Fiscal Capacity Analysis tools can help a local government maintain a clear perspective on current or impending distortions in fiscal condition.[5] Given the relative ease in conducting such an analysis, the burden for maintaining an ongoing review of fiscal health should be minimal. It is expected that this ability to monitor fiscal condition, preferably on an annual basis, will prove to be a cost-effective method of proactively maintaining fiscal health and fiscal direction long into the future.

As with any type of fiscal analysis, extraordinary circumstances unique to the local government can easily explain what at first glance may seem to be an alarming analytical result. Consequently, Chapter 7 focuses on how one can provide a more robust analysis of fiscal condition by incorporating the full context of fiscal issues surrounding the local government.

DISCUSSION QUESTIONS

1. How many years of data are required to conduct an analysis using the three tools outlined in this chapter?

2. What benefits can be realized by performing a multiyear analysis of the Ten-Point Test?

3. Why would the analyst prefer to partition the data set from GFOA into regions or population-sized categories as opposed to using the entire data set in aggregate to perform relative comparisons?

4. Distinguish between absolute and relative value. Which type of value does each of the tools use? What are the

---

[5] For another example of integrating the Ten-Point Test and the FTMS, see Faas and Parnerkar, 1999.

advantages and disadvantages of employing either method?

5. Discuss the necessity of adjusting for inflation. Why is it required for some calculations of trends and not for others?

6. What utility is derived from establishing a 5 percent threshold in the Fiscal Capacity Analysis as opposed to analyzing of larger classifications of revenues and expenditures? Might there be a more preferred budgetary threshold for some local governments? Why?

7. The tools presented in this chapter can be helpful for framing discussion and debate about local government policies. Suppose a local government has accepted discretionary federal grants for particular programs or expenditures. If this grant has a maximum length of time a jurisdiction can receive this funding, how should the local government prepare for the eventual termination of these external funds? Will the local government drop the funded service when funds dry up? Will the local government pick up the tab in the wake of the federal subsidy? Will the public come to expect the deeper level of service made possible through the infusion of intergovernmental aid so local officials have no choice but to continue funding with local resources?

References

Alter, T. R., McLaughlin, D. K., and Melniker, N. E. (no date). *Analyzing Local Government Fiscal Capacity*, Pennsylvania State University Cooperative Extension Service, University Park, PA.

Brown, K. W. (1996). *Ten-Point Test of Financial Condition with Comparative Ratios for Counties*, Springfield, MO: Solstice Productions.

———. (1993). The 10-Point Test of financial condition: Toward an easy-to-use assessment tool for smaller cities, *Government Finance Review*, 9 (6), 21–26.

Faas, R. C., and Parnerkar, I. D. (1999). *Tools for Analyzing the Fiscal Capacity of Local Governments*, A Presentation to the 33rd Annual Pacific Northwest Regional Economic Conference., Washington State University.

Groves, S. M., and Valente, M. G. (1994). *Evaluating Financial Condition: A Handbook for Local Government*, 3rd ed. Washington, DC: International City/County Management Association.

Honadle, B. W., and Lloyd-Jones, M. (1998). Analyzing rural local governments' financial condition: An exploratory application of three tools, *Public Budgeting and Finance*, 69–85.

———. University-local government collaboration to study fiscal health, *Government Finance Review*, 51–52.

Appendix A: Adjusting for Inflation

This adjustment will be necessary for all trends outlined in the Fiscal Capacity Analysis tool as well as some of those used in the FTMS. Inflation adjustment essentially follows a simple five-step process.

1. Identify a price deflator index.

2. Select a base year.

3. Adjust price deflator to selected base year.

4. Divide adjusted price deflator by 100.

5. Apply the price deflator to nominal values.

Example: Step 1: Identifying a Price Deflator
A number of governmental and economic research organizations publish price deflators. These deflators are commonly used to adjust Gross Domestic Product from nominal to real or "inflation-adjusted" values. Doing so allows for meaningful comparisons of monetary values over long periods. Such an adjustment to real values is critical when an analyst performs trend analysis. For illustration purposes, the implicit price deflator from the U.S. Department of Commerce is chosen. This deflator can be found in *The Survey of Current Business*, which is published monthly by the Department of Commerce.

Implicit Price Deflator: 1990–1997

Year	Deflator Index (1992 = 100)
1990	93.6
1991	97.3
1992	100.0
1993	102.6
1994	105.1
1995	107.8
1996	110.2
1997	112.4

Source: U.S. Department of Commerce

Step 2: Selecting a Base Year

The deflators for the years 1990–1997 are reported in a 1992-based year. It is recommended that the analyst select a base year that closely matches the time period under study by the local government. If the base year in which the deflator is reported is satisfactory, then one need not perform steps 1 through 3 in this appendix. For our purposes, we convert the base year to **1994**.

Step 3: Adjust Price Deflator to Selected Base Year

The price deflator as reported from the Department of Commerce can be converted from a base year of 1992 to 1994 via the following method:

- Set base year = 100
- Modify each subsequent year using following formula:

Adjusted deflator for current year = (Adjusted deflator for previous year) × (Unadjusted deflator for current year) / (Unadjusted deflator for previous year)

Year	Deflator (1992 = 100)	Calculation	Adjusted Deflator (1994 = 100)
1994	105.1	N/A	100.0
1995	107.8	(100.0*107.8)/105.1 =	102.6
1996	110.2	(102.6*110.2)/107.8 =	104.9
1997	112.4	(104.9*112.4)/110.2 =	106.9

Step 4: Divide Adjusted Price Deflator by 100

Year	Deflator (1994 = 100)	Deflator / 100
1994	100	1.000
1995	102.6	1.026
1996	104.9	1.049
1997	106.9	1.069

Step 5: Application of the Price Deflator to Nominal Values

Divide nominal dollars to inflation-adjusted dollars by dividing nominal value in a given year by the adjusted deflator for that same year. In this example we convert total revenues in nominal values to inflation adjusted values for 1994 base year.

	Total Revenues (Nominal)	Calculation	Total Revenues (Real, Inflation Adj.)
1994	$106,465,054	N/A	$106,465,054
1995	$108,512,020	$108,512,020 / 1.026	$105,762,202
1996	$110,625,253	$110,625,253 / 1.049	$105,457,820
1997	$112,323,724	$112,323,724 / 1.069	$105,073,643

The difference in making this critical adjustment is graphically illustrated in Figure A.1 using revenue data from Step 5.

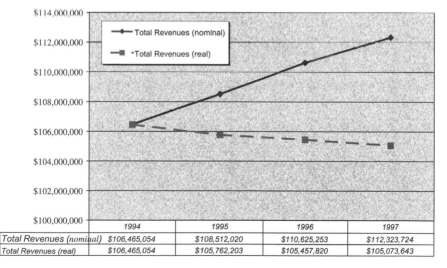

	1994	1995	1996	1997
Total Revenues (nominal)	$106,465,054	$108,512,020	$110,625,253	$112,323,724
Total Revenues (real)	$106,465,054	$105,762,203	$105,457,820	$105,073,643

Figure A.1   *Total Revenues (real vs. nominal)*

One can clearly see from this hypothetical example in Figure A.1 the need to make adjustment for inflation. Not doing so might lead the reader to the false conclusion that revenues have exhibited a steady increase over the period 1994–1997. Knowing better might focus your attention on the underlying causes of this apparent real decline.

SEVEN
Analysis and Interpretation

$\mathbf{A}$ thorough analysis of local government finance is best conducted in a holistic fashion, where inputs taken from many sources are thoughtfully incorporated into a comprehensive assessment of fiscal health. Inputs to consider may be either quantitative (as in the three methods discussed in Chapter 6) or qualitative (as reflected by educated views and personal experiences of residents from the local community).

This chapter focuses on analysis with interpretation rather than just quantitative methods or straightforward numerical assessment. The difference between the two approaches to fiscal health analysis can mean the difference between a generic representation of local government finances, one that could seemingly have been conducted in a near automated fashion, and one that is a true representation of the complete fiscal condition of the local government. The latter will most surely result only when the financial and demographic data not only are manipulated to calculate ratios and reveal trends but also are enriched by the significant input resulting from frequent interaction with local government officials and long-time residents.

Numerous quantitative measures are discussed in this chapter. All are derived by using the three tools presented in the preceding chapter. Throughout this chapter application of the three tools and interpretation of their results will revolve around examples from case studies of three fictitious local governments, each government comprised of a different economic base, population demographics, and consequently each with its own unique set of fiscal challenges. Accompanying those measures is a brief summary of the context of the local government. As the methods outlined in Chapter 6 are put into practice, the reader is encouraged to consider the importance of local government context when interpreting the analytical results from the three tools.

CASE STUDY I: GLENDON COUNTY

The first case study is of "Glendon County." A brief description of Glendon County would characterize it as a medium-sized county of approximately 22,000 residents in the heart of the Grain Belt. Being a heavily agricultural community, Glendon has long benefited from the price protection afforded its predominantly farming residents by the federal government for production of select agricultural commodities. Consequently, its economy has been relatively strong over the years, although population demographics for Glendon fall in line with a national trend indicating that fewer and larger farms are needed today with fewer workers needed to operate them. This trend is confirmed by the fact that the fastest growing segment of the population in Glendon are those 50 years and older. That statistic coupled with the knowledge that the population overall is exhibiting a slow downward trend, with more of its youth leaving the county for employment opportunities in large urban centers outside of Glendon than entering, and the long-term viability of Glendon's economy as it stands today starts to become less certain.

Consider the following two indicators from the Financial Trend Monitoring System (FTMS): both Figure 7.1 and Figure 7.2 show growth in revenues and expenditures that are approximately equal, about 5 percent growth per annum. Although both measures are steadily increasing over time, given that relative

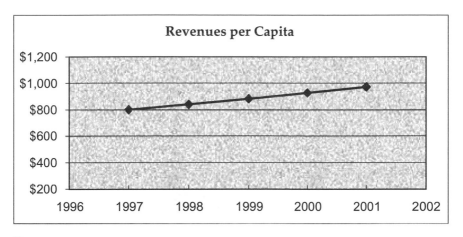

FIGURE 7.1

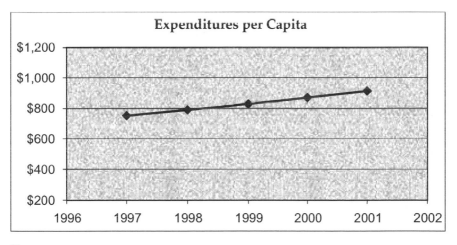

FIGURE 7.2

parity exists between the two, these measures considered together do not provide a cause for concern. In Figure 7.3, we see a historical plot of intergovernmental revenues over the last five years. Intergovernmental revenues include revenue sources such as highway aids, shared revenues, and short-term grant money, some of which are often subject to the political preferences of changing state and national government administrations.

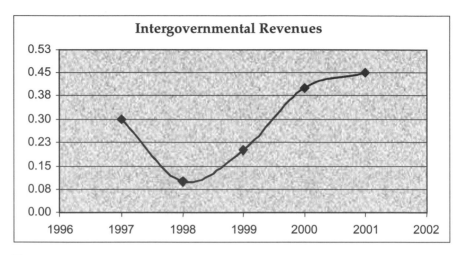

FIGURE 7.3

Consequently, they are not guaranteed to be in place for years to come. As such, this source of revenues should always be used with its relative impermanent nature in mind.

A strong upward trend is visible in this segment of total revenues. A logical next question might be to what extent is the growth in revenues per capita seen in Figure 7.1 driven by the dramatic growth in intergovernmental revenues? A quick look at ratio 2 from the Ten-Point Test, *Total General Fund Revenues from Own Sources/Total General Fund Revenues*, provides just the insight needed to answer this question.

Table 7.1 tells us that on a relative comparison basis, Glendon County is heavily reliant on intergovernmental revenues to fund government operations. What together appeared to be a sign of controlled growth exhibited in Figure 7.1 and Figure 7.2 now shows signs of vulnerability. That is, when the revenue streams are examined more closely, the sustainability of the 5 percent growth in expenditures now appears to be in question.

Now consider the debt profile of Glendon County. Table 7.2 depicts a chart of both the total debt per capita and the debt

TABLE 7.1

Ratio # 2	Year	Ratio	Score
Total General Fund Revenues from Own	1997	0.746	−1
Sources/Total General Fund Revenues	1998	0.778	−1
	1999	0.812	0
	2000	0.753	−1
	2001	0.714	−1

TABLE 7.2

Ratio # 9	Year	Ratio	Score
Direct Long-Term Debt/Population	1997	$13.50	2
	1998	$25.80	2
	1999	$28.30	2
	2000	$21.40	2
	2001	$15.90	2
Ratio # 10			
Debt Service/Total Revenues	1997	0.001	2
	1998	0.001	2
	1999	0.002	2
	2000	0.001	2
	2001	0.001	2

service burden expressed as ratios 9 and 10 from the Ten-Point Test. Recall from the previous chapter that a score of [+]2 indicates a sign of relative strength when compared with other counties in the GFOA database.

We see that for all five years studied, Glendon County earned a [+]2 for both ratios 9 and 10. High marks for these two indicators undoubtedly will contribute to a favorable overall ranking when the other 8 ratios of this test are calculated. While this initially appears to be a positive sign, we find that such high marks are the result of an exceptionally low level of outstanding long-term debt and accordingly very low level of principal and interest payments to service that debt. Suppose that through discussions about this apparent data anomaly with local government officials, we learn that Glendon has adopted a standing policy of strongly discouraging the use of long-term debt to finance capital expenditures. This revelation brings a new dimension to the analysis, a philosophical debate over the appropriate use of debt. At this point traditional analytical methods of fiscal health analysis via quantitative tools leave us with nothing to offer in terms of guidance. Nonetheless, thoughtful consideration of this long-standing policy can help frame the debate and still add value to the overall assessment of fiscal condition.

While this is largely a local decision, it is worth noting that financing all capital outlays with cash, the necessary consequence of rejecting the use of debt, will most surely limit the growth potential of the county. This limitation stems from the fact that any significant capital improvement not only is extraordinarily expensive, but also will likely rise in cost as the government waits to accumulate sufficient liquid assets to pay for the outlay upfront. In addition, this pay-as-you-go philosophy raises questions about the inequitable assessment of tax burden on the payers of the project versus the beneficiaries. Those who have paid may not be physically present to benefit from its use once the intended use of the capital is in place. The beneficiaries of capital expenditures may be future generations or newcomers to the community.

So now the residents of Glendon must weigh the benefits of the "no-risk no-debt" approach, against the possible opportunity costs of delayed or stunted economic expansion and the meager rates of growth the all-cash philosophy dictates. An added dimension to the analysis is the hard realization that the population of Glendon is aging and decisions that either protect that aging population from undue financial hardship or attract the influx of a younger taxpaying populous must be considered. In that light, arguments can now be made to support either side of the debt management debate.

Case Study II: Sharpelle County

The second case study focuses on a different but equally challenging set of economic circumstances. In "Sharpelle County," pains of urban sprawl and prospects of economic prosperity place a unique set of strains on the fiscal health of this local government. Sharpelle sits on the periphery of a bustling metropolis that has experienced one of the South's most rapid rates of expansion. As the suburbs continue to encircle the metropolitan core in a series of concentric rings, opportunities to establish light industry, residential subdivisions, and all of associated modern conveniences of suburban life find themselves well placed in Sharpelle. The challenge for local officials in Sharpelle is to determine what rate of expansion is optimal, and how to manage that expansion in such a way that the fiscal health of its community is not placed in jeopardy.

We begin by returning to two of the broadest measures of fiscal condition, revenues and expenditures per capita. See Figure 7.4 and Figure 7.5. A casual look at the rates of growth between revenues and expenditures immediately reveals an imbalance between the two in favor of expenditures. In and of itself, this imbalance does not seem to be a sustainable situation. Next let us turn our attention to a smaller segment of expenditures to see if we can identify any of its drivers. A review of line items in the budget not exceeding 5 percent of total revenues, as prescribed by the Fiscal Capacity Analysis, should help to isolate categories responsible for this growth in expenditures.

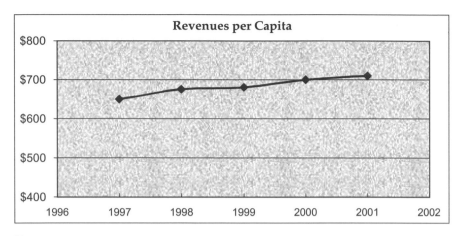

FIGURE 7.4

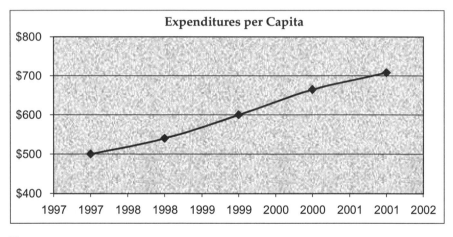

FIGURE 7.5

As depicted in Figures 7.6 through 7.8, we see that expenditures on economic development have experienced a rapid rate of increase. Given the growth environment for Sharpelle described previously, expenditures such would seem to be not only necessary but also prudent to ensure the proper management of its expanding business base. Also demonstrating a strong upward trend are the graphs of expenditures on Streets and Highways

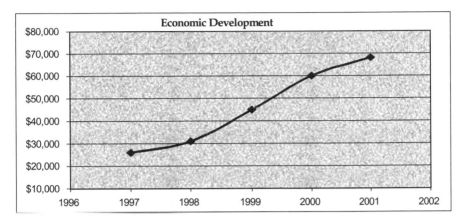

Figure 7.6

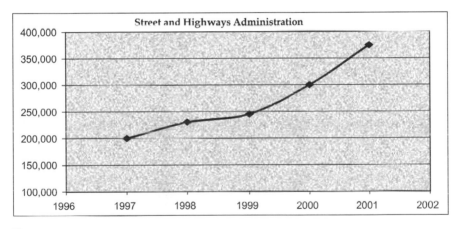

Figure 7.7

Administration (Figure 7.7) and Public Safety (Figure 7.8). Again, these trends seem to be the natural consequence of a growing community as it manages its infrastructure and polices its growing population.

A review of the debt profile for Sharpelle will likely depict a situation quite unlike that seen in the agricultural community of Glendon County described in Case Study I. A look at the debt structure ratios from the Ten-Point Test will provide insight into

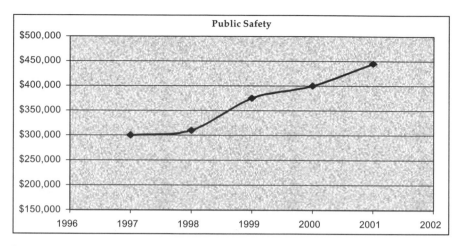

FIGURE 7.8

TABLE 7.3

Ratio # 9	Year	Ratio	Score
Direct Long-Term Debt/Population	1997	$41.37	1
	1998	$42.18	1
	1999	$45.32	0
	2000	$47.01	0
	2001	$48.25	−1
Ratio # 10			
Debt Service/Total Revenues	1997	0.0080	2
	1998	0.0074	1
	1999	0.0130	0
	2000	0.0260	−1
	2001	0.0260	−1

how this expansion is being managed. Table 7.3 shows the trend of relative scores for ratios 9 and 10 of the Ten-Point Test.

In Table 7.3 we see that Sharpelle's scores have deteriorated over the last two years. Clearly, the County is taking on more debt to facilitate the expansion of its infrastructure and hence to enable the overall growth of its community. Thus, a strategic decision was made to use debt in this fashion based on the belief, and hopefully strong supporting evidence, that economic growth prospects were solid and thus warranted the extra debt burden on the community.

Taken as a whole, the seemingly numerous signs of fiscal strain on Sharpelle would suggest a government in financial trouble. However, as an analyst armed with rich context of numerous background details, the imbalance in expenditures and revenues, accompanied by the surge in levels of spending on police, infrastructure, and economic development, combined with the relatively high debt load, all appear to be short-term in nature and therefore nothing more than the pains of a rapidly growing community revealing themselves in the fiscal indicators of the three tools. Had the quantitative indicators for Sharpelle *not* been supported by the backdrop of such an optimistic local economic climate, these very same results would clearly send warning signs of impending fiscal trouble for any other community.

Case Study III: The City of Meirwood

The preceding case studies should demonstrate the benefit of supporting one's analytical results within the context of local government conditions complemented by expert knowledge and insight from local officials. The importance of interpreting quantitative measures in this manner can prevent one from developing a rather inaccurate view; a view that would raise red flags and sound alarms all for nothing, or conversely a view that misses an impending fiscal crisis altogether. Occasionally, however, the fiscal strain is so acute that quantitative measures alone may provide an accurate representation of fiscal condition.

Consider the case of Meirwood. In a departure from the format of the previous two case studies, selected results from the three tools will be presented first and then the characterization and context of the local government will follow. Doing so will provide a confirmation or possibly invalidation of the initial impression left by the three tools.

Figure 7.9 (Governmental Funds) is a graphic depiction of revenues used to finance most governmental operations ranging from general purpose, to special revenue, to debt service, and capital projects. In Figure 7.9, a clear decline is seen in this broad indicator of primary funding source to facilitate government operations. Figure 7.10 shows expenditures on the critical services

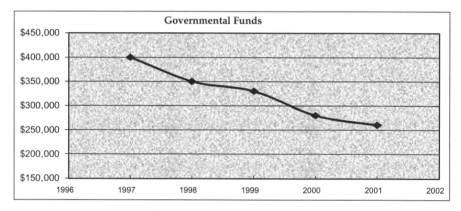

FIGURE 7.9

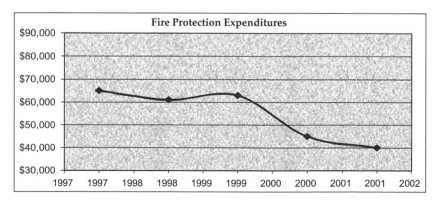

FIGURE 7.10

of the Meirwood Fire Department. Witnessing this sharp decline begs the question of whether adequate protection services are still being provided in light of the persistent decline in fire expenditures. In Figure 7.11, we see expenditures on sanitation steadily increasing likely due to the ongoing maintenance and increasing expense required of an aging sanitation system. A look at the tax base of the City of Meirwood is provided by the FTMS shown in Figure 7.12 and Figure 7.13.

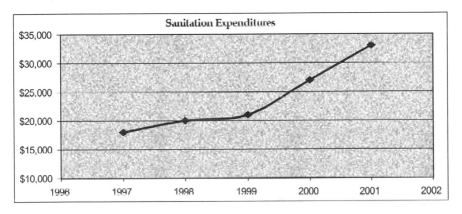

FIGURE 7.11

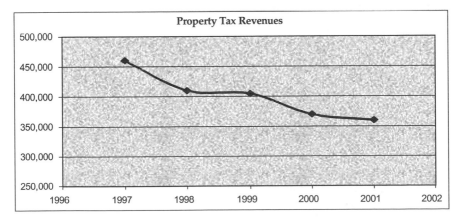

FIGURE 7.12

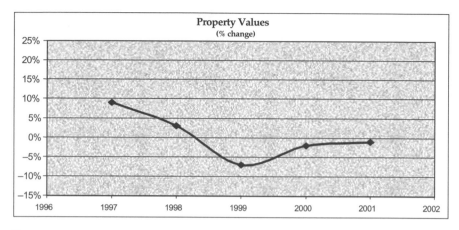

FIGURE 7.13

A marked decline in property tax revenues is accompanied by a decline in rate of change in property values. The latter is perhaps more meaningful because it may suggest that a fundamental economic problem is at hand for the local economy. Clearly a drop in tax revenues cannot be countered without imposing a tremendous tax burden if the underlying property values themselves are falling.

With declining revenues, rising expenses for sanitation, and cutbacks in support of fire protection services, one might wonder if ongoing maintenance of other services such as roads, bridges, ditches, and utilities are also falling by the wayside in Meirwood. A look at ratio 4 of the Ten-Point Test provides a general indication as to the maintenance of the overall infrastructure (see Table 7.4).

The trend of ratio 4 (Operating Expenditures/Total Expenditures) is one of relatively poor performance for a city of this size. Considering that ¯1 is the lowest possible score a ratio can receive, a mix of 0's and ¯1's is not a sign of health. As suspected, such weak scores hint at troubles for adequate maintenance of the infrastructure for Meirwood. Also in Table 7.4 we see in ratio 7 (Total General Fund Liabilities/Total General Fund Revenues)

TABLE 7.4

Ratio # 4	Year	Ratio	Score
Operating Expenditures/Total	1997	0.872	0
Expenditures	1998	0.861	0
	1999	0.926	−1
	2000	0.885	0
	2001	0.992	−1
Ratio # 7			
Total General Fund Liabilities/Total	1997	14.37	2
General Fund Revenues	1998	2.65	0
	1999	2.33	0
	2000	5.84	1
	2001	1.92	−1

a pattern of deteriorating strength in the ability of the city to meet short-term obligations with cash reserves.

All in all, a consistent negative message is being sent by the quantitative assessment of the three tools. When we examine the economic profile of this city, we find that Meirwood is an isolated community in a remote part of the state. A former manufacturing town of specialty apparel, Meirwood's major employers have since left the city to pursue lower wage opportunities overseas for their operations. Being a border city, it also contends with the competition provided by the business community in a neighboring state, where the business climate is much more tax friendly. Consequently, Meirwood has been losing small businesses and jobs steadily over the years to towns over the border. Furthermore, we find that Meirwood's population is on a consistent downward track and that little opportunity exists in this community to attract new residents. It appears as though Meirwood, although once a prosperous community, has fallen victim to changing economic times and has been unable to transform itself in the face of its geographic and business competitive disadvantages.

In this situation, although the overall sad state of affairs is likely apparent to all residents in the city of Meirwood, it is often the case that without a formal analytical representation of the problem, no meaningful progress can begin, or tough decisions be made without hard and fast results provided by a comprehensive review of fiscal condition. In that case, even this straightforward representation of a grim picture can be the start of progress toward a strategic and well-planned reversal of an otherwise negative economic and fiscal scenario.

In conclusion, the value added to the analysis by "tying together" the various signals of fiscal health (whether they be trends, ratios, population demographics, or simply anecdotal evidence from local officials) can be significant. The ability to enrich the analysis by making such linkages is what differentiates a seemingly unrelated collection of graphs and charts from a well-constructed story of the recent history of the government's fiscal condition, a story that when carefully read is likely to be the best signal of what lies ahead.

DISCUSSION QUESTIONS

1. List potential sources of relevant information available to the analyst when conducting an analysis of fiscal health.

2. In what ways can qualitative information enter the analysis of fiscal health such that the findings from the three tools reflect the local context of the subject government?

3. What factors influencing fiscal condition may not be directly apparent in the findings of the three tools but may drive the results or otherwise add value to the analysis?

4. How can information derived from the three tools be used to develop popular presentations for the public review? For example, do any of the findings lend themselves to press releases, a public presentation, or an annual report to the citizens?

5. How might local officials use the results of these tools to make a case for increased taxes, lowered spending, debt financing, or other strategic shifts in composition of public finances?

EIGHT

Fiscal Effects of Local Government Boundary Adjustments[1]

When a local government's boundaries are changed through consolidation or annexation (and from the opposite perspective, detachment) local finances are affected. The focus of this chapter is the effects of local government boundary adjustments on local finances. This topic deserves special consideration because boundary adjustments are so common and their fiscal implications are complex and sometimes unexpected.

MIXED LESSONS FROM EXPERIENCE

Recall from Chapter 1 that local governments have varying degrees of control over factors that might impact their fiscal health for better or for worse. How much a particular type of local government is in a position to control or influence these boundary adjustments depends on individual state policies. In Ohio, for example, cities have traditionally had a lot more power over annexations than did the townships from which they gained

[1] Portions of this chapter are taken, with permission of the publisher, from Beth Walter Honadle, Projecting the Public Services and Finance Implications of Municipal Consolidation: Evidence from a Small-City Consolidation Study, *The Regionalist*, 3, 1/2 (Fall 1998), 41–53.

territory. Under a state law enacted in 2001, townships not only have more say in annexation proceedings, but also may be eligible for "reparations" due them for lost revenues for several years after an annexation. These new provisions were so unpalatable to one group of Ohio cities that they launched a petition drive to try to repeal the statute. So the revenue implications of boundary adjustments are not insignificant in the political arena.

One argument often used in favor of local government consolidation is that it will enhance local government finances. There is no question that some consolidation advocates actually believe that consolidation will improve the revenue-cost picture for their local government. Others may not be as sure of this benefit, but know that it is a good selling point to potential detractors. In fact, some observers have suggested that consolidation advocates are frequently motivated by other considerations, such as more or better services, and that they know that consolidation will, in fact, escalate local government expenditures. Sometimes the impetus for consolidation is more political, such as changing the power base of a community through the redrawing of jurisdictional boundaries.

In other words, as two scholars (Benton and Gamble, 1984, p. 191) studying city/county consolidation observed:

> *Although much of the reform literature and consolidation rhetoric suggests that consolidation is likely to save money and reduce taxes, the actual relationship between city/county consolidation and 'efficiency' is an empirical question.*

They found that economic forces are much more likely to determine local government revenue and expenditure policies. Other researchers (Breen, Costa, and Hendon, 1986) used cost-revenue analysis to estimate the expected revenue from annexation and compared those amounts with anticipated service costs. Using a case study of the Village of Middlefield, Ohio, they investigated the economic feasibility for annexing different types of land uses into a small municipality. Their work posits an eventual trade-off between a municipality's land and population growth and the quality of life in the community. They use different circumstances to show how policies intended to improve municipalities' cost-revenue ratios at the particular point in time can work against the community in the long run.

Condrey (1994) examined the organizational and personnel effects of the Athens-Clarke County, Georgia, consolidation. In that case, he found that the efficiencies achieved were due more to the political desire to cut spending than from the merging of two governments. Because of this political will, efficiencies might have occurred independent of consolidation. He listed several questions that future consolidation studies should ask, including what opportunities for efficiencies exist through consolidation, whether the opportunities for efficiencies are real, and whether the personnel systems and pay practices of the two governments are similar enough that equal pay issues will not arise (Condrey, p. 382).

Bunch and Strauss (1992) analyzed nine small towns near Pittsburgh, Pennsylvania, and simulated the effects of a consolidation on some of the towns. Many of the suggested managerial reforms (e.g., raising user fees, using volunteer firefighters, etc.) were actually adopted by the towns as a result of their study, but none of the towns consolidated and they continued to incur annual operating fiscal deficits.

A GENERAL FRAMEWORK

Every proposed municipal consolidation has unique aspects. Local history, citizen preferences, demographics, opportunities for utilizing excess capacity or removing duplication, state institutional and legal structures, and other specific details vary from case to case. Despite these important differences, it helps to have a general framework for analyzing the fiscal implications of municipal expansions whether from annexations or consolidations. These include impacts on the following:

- *Intergovernmental financial aids:* Virtually all local governments receive some intergovernmental aids. If the type and amount of aid would be affected by a consolidation, such expected changes should be studied.
- *Debt burdens:* If either jurisdiction has outstanding general obligation debt, it is appropriate to consider how spreading the debt over the taxpayers in a merged jurisdiction would affect taxpayers' liabilities. This consideration should be weighed (by politicians or voters) against the perceived benefits all of the residents will receive from the investments purchased with the debt. (Again, how outstanding debt is handled after consolidation will vary from state to state.)
- *Tax rates:* The tax rates in the two jurisdictions should be compared with the expected tax rate in the consolidated jurisdiction to project how tax bills will be changed if the consolidation passes.
- *Other jurisdictions:* Boundary adjustments also may affect overlapping jurisdictions such as school districts and special districts. It is important to analyze how the services and associated costs for these other jurisdictions would be affected, if at all, by consolidation.
- *Costs associated* with the *status quo:* If maintaining the *status quo* (i.e., maintaining two separate local governments or not annexing certain property) entails recurring costs, then these expenditures must be considered.
- *Local service costs:* It is important to consider the likely impact of consolidation on the cost of providing local services. Analysis requires a detailed description of

current functions and budgets for each jurisdiction and careful consideration of opportunities for streamlining. If one of the cities has excess capacity for a particular service (such as unused sewage treatment capacity or water storage capacity, idle space, underutilized equipment), it might be appropriate to extend this service to the other jurisdiction so the cost can be shared more economically for both parties. However, if both cities were already at capacity, consolidation would not be expected to lead to more efficiency.

- *Particular segments of the population*: For equity reasons, particular segments of the population (special interests) may need to have their circumstances analyzed separately. This could be citizens in certain geographic areas, low-income persons, minorities, or other identifiable segments of the population in a particular case who might be unduly harmed by consolidation.

A CASE EXAMPLE

We present a rather detailed case study of an actual consolidation to show how the fiscal effects of the consolidation were projected and what actually happened after consolidation occurred. It is presented to show how a simple, straightforward analysis can be done and to illustrate the impossibility of making precise, accurate predictions beforehand. This inability to make projections with absolute certainty is inevitable because the newly elected government of a consolidated city will have the discretion to cut expenditures or spend a lot more on new and better services. Also, unanticipated changes in state aids, energy prices, mandated expenditures, and so on will occur and render the projection either too high or too low.

Does this mean we are saying that communities should not even try to project the effects of local boundary adjustments on finances because the projections are bound to be off? Not at all. It does mean that care should be taken to present some likely scenarios of what might happen so that decision makers can exercise informed judgment about whether to support the consolidation. It is important to emphasize that all the analyst can do is project the effects of the boundary adjustment itself on finances. How finances change will be a function not only of the boundary adjustment, but also of political, economic, institutional, and social factors, including changes in the demand for local services.

This case study involves two small cities in eastern central Minnesota, Branch and North Branch. The Branch-North area was rapidly growing as a result of its commuting distance (under 50 miles) to the twin cities of Minneapolis and St. Paul, and there were increasing demands for services by businesses and citizens in Branch. North Branch could expand only through concurrent detachment and annexation of portions of Branch. This was because Branch, Minnesota, with a 1990 population of 2,400, was a six-mile by six-mile square that completely encircled North Branch and its 1,866 inhabitants. North Branch was slightly over one square mile in area.

At the time of the proposed consolidation (1992), North Branch was largely developed with residential areas, a main street, and industry. Branch had no main street, scattered residential development with much of its population near the North Branch border, little industry, and farms. North Branch provided water, sewer, police protection, and other services to its residents, while Branch was more like a rural township and contracted for municipal services. The two city governments historically were mutually antagonistic for reasons of annexation disputes and personal antipathies, making interlocal governmental cooperation between them virtually nonexistent. From a list of 22 facilities and services compiled by the Branch—North Branch Consolidation Study Commission, Branch provided 11, contracted/provided 9, and did not supply 2; North Branch provided 19, contracted 2, and did not supply 1. Branch contracted out many services. Only recently had it hired a full-time city administrator.

THE PREDICTION

The commission always assumed that public finance was the most important question. For the residents of Branch and North Branch to decide whether to support consolidation of the two cities, they needed to understand the impact of consolidation on:

1. Intergovernmental financial aid
2. The distribution of outstanding debt repayment
3. Property taxes
4. The North Branch Area Independent School District
5. Costs associated with detachment and annexation
6. Local service costs
7. Rural residents

These are addressed in turn.

INTERGOVERNMENTAL AID IMPACT

The commission focused considerable attention on the likely consequences of consolidation for intergovernmental aids, especially state aid, given its importance to the two local governments and their taxpayers.

The commission made numerous assumptions. One assumption was that the state aid formulas would not change. Given the state legislature's frequent changes in intergovernmental aid formulas, that particular assumption likely would not hold forever. However, the only way to understand the impact of *consolidation* on finances was to hold such influential factors constant since consolidation did not affect these variables.

The commission also assumed that the combined population of Branch and North Branch would soon reach 5,000 (an assumption since borne out), the threshold for Minnesota local governments to start receiving financial aids for local roads. Again, the underlying assumption was that the state would not change its policy of giving road aid to cities of 5,000 and over in population. Since it was clear that the population was growing so rapidly that the combined population would make the cutoff at the time of consolidation, it would not have been appropriate to assume that their population would be under 5,000.

The commission found that one form of aid (Homestead and Agricultural Credit Aid, a form of property tax relief in Minnesota) would be unaffected by consolidation. However, another type of financial aid (for general purposes), local government aid (LGA), would be reduced by the consolidation: Once a city's population reached 2,500, the city would fall under a less lucrative LGA formula than smaller cities in Minnesota. Because Branch would be reaching that population soon, even without consolidation, consolidation would merely accelerate the process by which Branch would be receiving fewer general-purpose LGA dollars.

In the short run, then, the consolidated city would receive $11,113 fewer LGA dollars by consolidating than if the two cities were to remain separate. This amounts to 5 percent less LGA flowing to the area (Branch—North Branch Consolidation Study Commission, 1994, p. 10).

On the inflow side, a consolidated city would immediately be eligible for road aid, which neither city was currently receiving. Moreover, since the threshold for receiving these dollars was a population of 5,000, neither city *alone* would stand to receive these funds for many years to come. The consolidated city would qualify at minimum for over $124,000 annually based on its population and street mileage.

Although the specifics of state aid will vary by state and the factors to qualify for those dollars will vary from locality to locality, the important point is to look at these aids comprehensively and make as reasonable assumptions as possible for predicting how intergovernmental aids will be affected by the boundary adjustment. Based on this analysis, one can be fairly confident in the net effect of the change on the fiscal picture of the community. And, as we saw in this case, the projection was for a modest decrease in general-purpose aid and a large increase in earmarked funds for roads. Knowing not only the level of change, but also whether the change affects types of expenditures will also be of interest to policy makers and taxpayers.

IMPACT OF CONSOLIDATION ON DEBT BURDEN

Under Minnesota's consolidation law, taxpayers in the areas of the former cities are liable for any outstanding debt unless the debt is combined before consolidation. The Branch and North Branch city councils would have had to pass resolutions supporting consolidation of the two cities' old debt before debt consolidation could occur.

The commission employed a two-step approach to analyzing the impact of consolidation on paying off old debt. It analyzed the debt of the two cities separately, and then estimated the impact of debt repayment on property taxes with the debt spread over the combined area of the former Branch and North Branch cities.

The debt question was particularly important in this case study because the prevailing perception in the community was that North Branch was heavily in debt and consolidation would lead to a sharp rise in Branch residents' property taxes to help pay off the other city's old debt.

The two-step analysis showed that North Branch had about $7 million in outstanding municipal debt compared to approximately $2 million for Branch. (North Branch had water and sewer systems largely financed by debt.) Approximately $2 million of North Branch's $7 million debt was in revenue bonds. Utility customers were repaying these, so only those who directly benefited from the debt-financed services contributed to paying off that debt. Of the remaining $5 million, about 80 percent of it was in special assessments.

Thus, Branch taxpayers would be liable for their share of the remainder about $1 million worth of municipal debt. The commission estimated that it would cost slightly under $30 per year per average taxpaying unit to pay off North Branch's old debt (excluding revenue bonds and special assessments). To calculate the "average taxpaying unit," the commission simply divided the amount of debt to be repaid in a given year by the number of property parcels on which taxes were to be paid. So, if the debt were merged, the taxpayers in old North Branch would have some extra help from new taxpayers to pay off the outstanding debt (for services old Branch residents would now get to enjoy as citizens in the consolidated community) and the taxpayers from old Branch would pay a relatively small amount to pay down the outstanding general obligation debt of old North Branch.

As it turned out, the former city councils chose not to pass resolutions consolidating the municipal general obligation debt prior to consolidation. But, had they chosen to merge the debt, this was how the commission had projected the debt would affect taxpayers in the jurisdictions.

PROPERTY TAX IMPACT

For several reasons, the commission could not make generalizations about whether residents' property tax bills would likely go up or down. Local property tax bills include not only municipal taxes, but also taxes levied by all of the property taxing units of local government. Also, property tax levies are affected by intergovernmental aids, changes in property values, mandates from higher levels of government, and other factors beyond the control of the local officials who levy their property taxes.

With these and other caveats, the commission provided information (with the help of the Chicago County auditor) on existing tax liabilities for residential and commercial properties for the two separate cities. It projected the merged jurisdiction's tax liabilities on commercial and residential properties.

The report contained a series of tables showing actual property tax liabilities for different market values of properties. First was a side-by-side comparison of property tax liabilities (before consolidation) for taxpayers in Branch and North Branch with properties of the same value. Then it showed variation in property tax liabilities given a combined two cities budget, and excised debt, and a tax liability assumed by both jurisdictions. A final variation showed changes in combined liabilities based both on savings from elimination of duplication and on revenues from state road aid.

Residents were able to see how consolidation *by itself* would affect their municipal property tax liabilities. Because the tables showed what would happen to a property tax bill if the budgets of the two cities were combined, the resulting property tax liabilities were dispersed over the large community, the road aid would be forthcoming, and certain automatic reductions in duplication would occur, such as half as many council members.

Post-consolidation, political philosophies or action might transform the assumptions in unforeseen ways. The newly elected city council could decide to spend more in certain areas, state aids could be reduced, new mandates could come down from above, property values could change, and so forth.

IMPACT ON NORTH BRANCH AREA SCHOOL DISTRICT

Branch and North Branch were served by the Independent School District (ISD) 138, the North Branch Area School

District, which would benefit fiscally from the consolidation in two ways. First, some of the North Branch public schools were physically located in Branch but were receiving utilities from adjacent North Branch. The school district was paying a higher nonresidential rate than it would pay if the cities were consolidated. Second, ISD 138 had spent thousands of dollars on legal fees for a proposed annexation to obtain water and sewer services at the lower, resident rate in North Branch.

IMPACT ON COSTS ASSOCIATED WITH DETACHMENT AND ANNEXATION

A minimum of $60,000 had been spent between the county, school district, and the cities of Branch and North Branch opposing and promoting annexation. If consolidation were to occur, no more public monies need be spent litigating the detachment of parcels of land from Branch and the annexation of them to North Branch. Typical was the 179 acres detached from Branch and annexed to North Branch during the commission's deliberations. The consolidation of the two cities would end the resultant expensive appeals.

IMPACT OF CONSOLIDATION ON LOCAL SERVICE COSTS

What would the effect of consolidation be on expenditures for general government and public services? The analysis began by showing what the two cities were currently spending for major categories of expenditure (separately) and summing these to show how much the communities were spending on these functions and services in total.

The commission deducted amounts reimbursed by earmarked intergovernmental revenues (e.g., amounts received for fire protection and police training) to present a more comparable set of expenditures from own-source revenues. Table 8.1 presents these net expenditures. It is debatable whether the "right" way to do

TABLE 8.1   *A Comparison of Expenditures (Excluding Earmarked Intergovernmental Aids) for Branch and North Branch, 1993*

Expenditure Category	Actual FY 1993	Aggregate	Expenditure Category
North Branch	Branch	Branch and North Branch Combined	
$154,000	$118,458	$272,458	General Government and Administration
247,314	164,785	412,099	Public Works
38,982	29,119	68,101	Parks and Recreation
129,600	39,000	168,600	Public Safety*
16,000	11,500	27,500	Community Development and Planning
28,218	19,190	47,408	Miscellaneous
$614,114	$382,052	$996,166	Total

* Public safety includes police, fire, animal control civic defense, traffic lights, and fire wardens.
Source: Branch—North Branch Consolidation Study Commission, 1994, p. 15.

the analysis was to deduct these earmarked expenditures from an academic perspective. However, since this analysis was done by citizens nominated by both cities, one could argue that it is the right way to do the analysis since they represent the perspective of those most affected by the outcome.

Conjectures on whether expenditures would go up or down in a new city were dicey, because fiscal policy would depend, in part, on the philosophies and actions of the new city council. The commission devised two hypothetical situations to provide a glimpse of how consolidation might affect expenditures, as shown in Table 8.2 and Table 8.3.

Table 8.2 represents the local expenditures reduction if the smaller of the two current general governments and administrations were eliminated. Table 8.3 depicts the local government

TABLE 8.2 *A Projected Local Expenditures Reduction Based on Elimination of Smaller Government*

Expenditure Category	Pre-Consolidation	Post-Consolidation	Impact
General Government and Administration	$272,458	$154,000	Save $118,458 (43%)
Public Works	412,099	412,099	No Change
Parks and Recreation	68,101	68,101	No Change
Public Safety*	168,600	168,600	No Change
Community Development and Planning	27,500	16,000	Save $11,500 (42%)
Miscellaneous	47,408	47,408	No Change
Total	$996,166	$866,208	Save $129,958 (13%)

* Public safety includes police, fire, animal control civic defense, traffic lights, and fire wardens.
Source: Branch—North Branch Consolidation Study Commission, 1994, p. 16.

expenditures reduction (as in Table 8.2) with the complement of a new full-time planner, an additional policy deputy, and an additional office clerk.

Based on these hypothetical situations, the commission concluded that both scenarios netted cost savings for the residents. Eliminating duplicate expenses created savings, but additional spending by the new, consolidated city would offset those economies.[2]

---

[2] As it turned out, the new city council created a number of new positions, which the commission could not have anticipated. This suggests that it might have been a good idea to show a third scenario under which cost savings through eliminating duplication would be more than matched by increased expenditures

TABLE 8.3   *Projected Local Expenditures Reduction Based on Elimination of Smaller Government and New Supplemental Staff**

Expenditure Category	Pre-Consolidation	Post-Consolidation	Impact
General Government and Administration	$272,458	$174,000	Save $98,458 (36%)
Public Works	412,099	412,099	No Change
Parks and Recreation	68,101	68,101	No Change
Public Safety**	168,600	208,600	$40,000 increase (24%)
Community Development and Planning	27,500	47,500	$20,000 increase (73%)
Miscellaneous	47,408	47,408	No Change
Total	$996,166	$957,708	Save $38,458 (4%)

* Assuming the costs of adding a full-time planner, a police deputy, and a clerk would be $20,000, $40,000, and $20,000, respectively.
** Public safety includes police, fire, animal control civic defense, traffic lights, and fire wardens.
Source: Branch—North Branch Consolidation Study Commission, 1994, p. 16.

IMPACTS ON FARMERS

Although farmers were a very small percentage of Branch's population, they owned significant acreage in Branch and were vocal about their concerns. Their special interests could be addressed in a consolidated city through establishment of an area water/sewer district, or dual rural and urban taxing districts, the commission concluded. In other words, the commission acknowledged that people with large acreage might be affected in adverse ways, but stopped short of projecting the impact on their taxes since it would depend on the services the new city provided in their areas and the new city could choose to tax those areas receiving fewer city services at a lower rate. We mention this aspect of the study to show that, even though rural property taxpayers are affected by the consolidation, there are instances in which the most the analyst can do is present options for consideration by the government that takes over after consolidation.[3]

THE REALITY

This section presents data on public finances, expenditures, and implementation in the city in the first few years following the consolidation. Again, the reader should note that while some changes are direct effects of consolidation, other changes are not attributable to the boundary adjustment.

INTERGOVERNMENTAL AID IMPACT

Table 8.4 shows intergovernmental aids flowing to the new North Branch since the consolidation. The consolidated city of North Branch now receives over $72,676 annually in state road aids, funds not received before consolidation. The consolidated city is eligible to receive $290,000 annually in road aids, but had not requested all of it in the first couple of years after consolidation occurred.

Consolidation also made the community eligible for temporary grants from the Minnesota Board of Government Innovation and Cooperation. Distribution through this grant program was begun in 1994 by the State of Minnesota to encourage the

---

[3] Ironically, the former city of North Branch had a rural taxing district, while Branch (the more rural of the two) did not. The unequal fiscal burden of this dichotomous system of two taxing districts could create great controversy because property taxpayers in urban sections would pay more. The consolidated city has not created rural and urban taxing districts.

TABLE 8.4   *Intergovernmental Aids*

Type of Aid	Actual 1995	Actual 1996	Budget 1997
Government Innovation and Cooperation Grant	$96,320	$96,320	$96,000
Local Government Aid (General Purpose)	209,153	244,812	236,122
Municipal State Road Aid*	None	72,676	72,500
Housing and Agricultural Credit Aid (State-Funded Property tax Relief)	238,664	214,825	15,489
Small Cities Development Grant	None	18,750	797,117
COPS Fast Grant (Federal Grant)	None	None	75,000

* 25% of state aid money is to be used for street maintenance.
Source: North Branch City Clerk.

elimination of governmental units by defraying some of the initial costs associated with implementing a consolidation.

These costs include merging computer and personnel systems, hiring a new city administrator, and facilitating the transition. The consolidated city of North Branch obtained over $90,000 a year for its first four years through this program. The state aid formula is based on population, placing North Branch in the $20 per capita range. This is the clearest example of a financial benefit that resulted directly from consolidation. However, it is not one that only became available by a unique program of the state just as this consolidation was occurring.

A decline in HACA (the state-financed program for local property tax relief) occurred, but it was unrelated to the consolidation. The consolidated city also received additional new grants, including a COPS Fast Grant (a federal program for hiring local police) and a Small Cities Development Grant. So, although we include these figures to show how the newly consolidated city fared fiscally after the consolidation, one should not draw the conclusion that consolidation was responsible for all of the benefits and costs that occurred subsequent to the boundary change.

On balance, the biggest gain in intergovernmental funds due to the consolidation is in Municipal State Aid for roads. Eventually this should amount to about $290,000 annually. This change, as predicted, was a direct benefit to the community from consolidation because the consolidation would make the new city large enough population-wise to qualify for these aids.

DEBT BURDEN

As stated earlier, the existing debt liabilities remained with the taxpayers of the two former cities who incurred the debt. Any new debt is borne by all of the property tax payers in the consolidated city.

In 1996 the consolidated city issued four new bonds. A general obligation water and sewer bond ($330,000) was issued to complete the sewer and water interconnect project joining the two former cities' water towers and sewer systems. Another $620,000 in bonds was issued to refund in advance some outstanding bonds for storm sewers and wastewater treatment infrastructure. Another general obligation Improvement Bond ($465,000) was issued for residential streets and to extend a street into an industrial park. The $330,000 bond for connecting the two former cities' water towers and sewer systems was the only debt incurred that was directly attributable to consolidation.

PROPERTY TAX IMPACT

Table 8.5 shows property tax rates for 1995, 1996, and 1997. The tax rate differentials for the two areas occurred because the two former cities have separate debt retirement burdens. As the commission predicted, the tax rate for former Branch city taxpayers rose slightly at the same time as the property tax rate for former

TABLE 8.5   *Property Tax Rates (Percentage of Taxable Value) for 1995, 1996, and 1997*

Type of Aid	1995	1996	1997
Old Branch	19.02%	18.49%	22.30%
Old North Branch	31.49%	26.20%	29.80%

Source: North Branch City Clerk.

TABLE 8.6   *Expenditures for 1995, 1996, and 1997 for the Consolidated City of North Branch*

	Actual FY 1995	Actual FY 1996	Budgeted FY 1997
General Government	$407,726	$384,886	$661,749
Public Safety, minus:			
Police Training Aid	295,708	406,952	484,514
Police Aid	650	645	650
Fire Aid	8,198	9,378	8,500
COPS Fast Grant	16,535	19,384	13,000
(federal grant)	0	18,750	75,000
Then equals	270,325	358,795	387,364
Public Works	334,927	419,928	510,996
Culture and Recreation	97,294	54,744	138,240
Miscellaneous	117,869	211,373	160,340
Total	$1,228,141	$1,429,726	$1,858,690

Source: North Branch City Clerk.

North Branch taxpayers declined slightly. Tax rates in the former Branch would have risen somewhat even if consolidation had not occurred because of natural growth impulses.

EXPENDITURES SINCE CONSOLIDATION

Table 8.6 shows actual expenditures for 1995 and 1996 and budgeted expenditures for 1997. The biggest expenditure increase was in general government. While public works expenditures dropped considerably after the consolidation, two factors offset those savings. One factor was the one-time expenditure necessitated during the transition from two cities to one city, such as the hiring of an interim administrator. The other factor was the hiring of new personnel by the leadership of the newly consolidated city.

STAFFING CHANGES

The newly consolidated city had to merge two staffs. After the consolidation, the city hired a "consolidation coordinator" with the special funds received for consolidating from the Minnesota Board of Government Innovation and Cooperation. He reviewed departments to develop an organization plan, met with employees, reviewed the comparable worth plan (a state mandate for ensuring pay equity) for the consolidated city, and from there determined how to fit all the employees into that plan. For instance, both cities had public works supervisors. One of them was given the title of public works director and the other became street foreman. Both cities had deputy clerks. One was given the title and duties of city clerk. The other became the city treasurer.

Table 8.7 compares the personnel structure of old Branch and old North Branch to the personnel structure of the consolidated city of North Branch. The consolidated city created six new full-time positions, changed some part-time positions to full-time, and added new part-time positions. These changes illustrate the particular discretionary changes a new city council can make that will have an effect on local spending, but they are not predictable by analysts trying to make educated guesses about how consolidation will affect finances.

SUMMARY AND CONCLUSIONS OF THE CASE STUDY

The Branch—North Branch public finance analysis of consolidation is instructive to other situations in which changes in local government boundaries are being considered. The list of

TABLE 8.7   *Personnel Structure of the Cities of Old North Branch, Branch, and the Consolidated North Branch*

Position	Old North Branch 1994 Salary	Old Branch 1994 Salary	New North Branch 1995 Salary	New North Branch 1997 Salary
Salaried Employees				
City Administrator	$33,948	$34,819	$43,500	$49,200
City Clerk	0	0	26,200	30,780
Deputy Clerk	23,982	23,080	0	0
City Treasurer	0	0	27,000	34,780
City Planner	25,750	0	35,000	35,020
Building Official	0	0	31,000	35,020
Account Clerk	9,984*	0	17,992	21,540
Staff Secretary	0	0	0	18,540
Police Chief	35,426	0	36,000	43,200
Police Sergeant	31,130	0	32,100	34,780
Police Officer	0	0	0	26,600
Police Officer	0	0	0	32,600
Policy Officer	0	0	0	24,600
Police Secretary	0	0	0	20,040
Public Works Director	34,420	21,715	36,500	41,020
Street Foremen	26,208	0	26,000	28,600
Park Foreman	0	0	27,310	28,600
Public Works Maintenance I	21,288	0	17,992	21,540
Public Works Maintenance II	0	0	0	18,540
Liquor Store Manager	25,000	0	26,000	30,780
TOTAL	$267,136	$79, 614	$382,594	$575,780
Hourly Employees				
Liquor Store Cashiers	$6.23–$7.46/ hour	0	$6.23–$7.68/ hour	$6.81–$7.91/ hour
Janitor (Approx. 4 hrs/wk)	$7.46/hour	$40 per time	$7.68/hour	$8.18/hour

Source: North Branch City Clerk.
* Part-Time.

considerations (e.g., impacts on other governmental units, debt repayment, intergovernmental aids impacts) can be modified for analyzing annexations, detachments, and other forms of local government boundary adjustments. Indeed, the same method has been used to study other proposed consolidation and annexation in Minnesota. Because each situation is unique, one should be careful about applications based on the experience presented here.

GENERAL CONSIDERATIONS

However, some interesting results bear universal consideration. First, the cost of general government did not decrease after consolidation. New hires were not offset by pink slips.

As derived from Table 8.7, the residents of the combined municipalities paid approximately $81 per person in municipal salaries in 1994 and $135 per person in 1997. This 1997 figure does not include new debt incurred in 1996 of $1,415,000, which translates to $332 per resident, without interest charges, at least some of which trace back to consolidation. Neither does this include the impending expense of purchasing a new city hall (despite once having three!).

Because the new city is rapidly growing, some of the new hiring and expenditures might have taken place in any case and cannot be causally linked to consolidation. Furthermore, consolidation did pull in new funding sources. Yet the figures examined suggest an uncomplicated conclusion: Consolidation costs more.

This case study has shown how two small cities implemented their consolidation. It provided a framework for projecting the fiscal and serviced impact of consolidation and validated the projections through post-consolidation events. The results show that it is possible to project the impacts of a municipal consolidation on public services and finance by using data from the former cities and making realistic assumptions. Although the emphasis in this case study was on the fiscal aspects of consolidation (because of the topic of this book), one should not conclude that these are the only important factors in deciding whether to make boundary adjustments. Fiscal considerations must be weighed along with other considerations and values.

DISCUSSION QUESTIONS

1. A manufacturing company is seeking to relocate a facility closer to its suppliers. It is considering one possible location just outside the city limits of a municipality. The company will move there only if it can connect to water and sewer services available from the city. The city proceeds to annex the land in order to attract the development and thereby expand the city's tax base. What are some of the fiscal costs and benefits you might consider in deciding whether this is a good idea? Do you think your perspective would be different if you were a taxpayer in the jurisdiction whose territory is being annexed to the neighboring city? How so?

2. Suppose it could be shown persuasively that merging two adjacent cities would save the taxpayers of both jurisdictions considerable sums of money. What other factors would you consider before deciding to recommend consolidation?

REFERENCES

Benton, J. E., and Gamble, D. (1984). City/county consolidation and economies of scale: Evidence from a time-series analysis in Jacksonville, Florida. *Social Science Quarterly, 65*, 190–198.

Breen, E., Costa, F. J., and Hendon, W. (1986). Annexation: An economic analysis: Whether a small village or town should annex adjacent land is a cost/revenue problem. *American Journal of Economics and Sociology, 45* (2), 159–172.

Bunch, B. S., and Strauss, R. (1992). Municipal consolidation: An analysis of the financial benefits for fiscally distressed small municipalities. *Urban Affairs Quarterly 17*, 615–629.

Condrey, S. E. (1994). Organizational and personnel impacts on local government consolidation: Athens-Clarke County, Georgia. *Journal of Urban Affairs 16* (4), 371–383.

NINE

Practical Strategies for Local Fiscal Health

There is an old expression that goes, when you're up to your der-rière in alligators it's hard to remember that your original objec-tive was to drain the swamp. When a local government finds itself in the midst of a fiscal crisis, it is likewise difficult for officials to engage in thoughtful discussion about long-term strategy. While officials will adopt strategies to cope with an immediate crisis, this is a reactionary approach born of necessity. Ideally, local gov-ernments will plot strategy during the good times to avoid serious fiscal problems later on. But regardless of a government's current financial situation, it is never a bad time for local governments to consider strategies for maintaining or improving their fiscal health.

It may be easier to think about the long-term implications of policy when resources are abundant. Frances Stokes Berry (1994) found in an empirical study that, under conditions of strong fiscal health, state agencies are more likely to engage in strategic plan-ning. While it is necessary for any agency under fiscal stress to plan and manage the crisis, in reality agencies with "abundant or slack resources are more likely than agencies in cash strapped condition to be innovators" (p. 323). Berry wrote (p. 327) ". . . [A] strong positive relationship existed between a state's fiscal health and the propensity of its agencies to adopt strategic planning." Her findings *supported the slack resources hypothesis that fiscally healthy agencies are more likely to be innovators in adopting strategic planning than are fiscally weak agencies, and suggest that state leaders do not use strategic planning as a cutback management tool, but rather, as a tool for establishing mission statements and priorities during relatively strong fiscal conditions (p. 327).*

Or, as Shelton and Albee (2000, p. 90) put it, "A good argument can be made that it is best to prepare for hard times during good times. Objectivity comes more easily when there is less urgency to the decision process."

A recently completed landmark study of the management capacity of all levels of government in the United States argued that financial management is the most important management system in government. Lessons from that study help to make the point that strategic approaches to maintaining fiscal health are beneficial. According to the study, "Long-term planning is the key to stronger financial management capacity and better performance. . . . Budgeting should take on a sharper, more strategic goal within organizations" (Beekman, 2003, p. 9).

Some research has focused on strategies local governments pursue under conditions of stress. A survey of city, county, and school district budget officers in Florida found that local governments adopt different strategies during a recession, which is temporary, than pursuant to statutory changes, which are more permanent. This study found that local governments are more likely to engage in expenditure reductions than in revenue-raising strategies, with cuts being across-the-board because the shortfalls are short-term. Additionally, the more labor-intensive the local government is, the more likely it is to engage in personnel reduction strategies than on approaches such as borrowing, service shedding, and automation (MacManus, 1993).

Another study looked specifically at productivity improvement as a strategy for addressing fiscal stress brought on by a tax limitation measure (Stipak and O'Toole, 1993). This study surveyed managers in Oregon school districts, cities, and counties to ascertain their responses to a state-imposed property tax limitation measure. It examined four ways in which local governments respond to stress: reducing services, raising revenues, improving productivity, and shifting service provision to others (also called load-shedding). The researchers found that city and county administrators emphasized reducing services, raising revenues, and improving productivity approximately equally as responses for fiscal stress. As in earlier research by the investigators in this study, they found that productivity practices varied by the type of local government, with cities much less favorable toward reducing services than either counties or school districts. Also, while half of the school districts used strategic planning as a management tool, only about one-quarter of the cities and one-third of the counties did so. The investigators on this study concluded that, "because local managers accept productivity improvement as an important strategy for responding to fiscal stress, fiscal stress could foster further development of productivity improvement methods" (Stipak and O'Toole, 1993, p. 111). While this may be making a virtue out of necessity, it does bring out the opportunity created by having no choice but to take action to alleviate fiscal stress.

Reschovsky suggests that there are four major strategies cities can undertake to reduce their total spending: (1) increasing efficiency or productivity, (2) cutting or freezing employee wages and benefits, (3) eliminating services, and (4) privatizing services (Reschovsky, 1997, pp. 457–459).

One study of fiscal austerity responses by local governments found that intergovernmental structure affects the impact of particular fiscal management strategies. An international group of researchers compared local governments in unitary systems (France, Finland, and Denmark) and federal systems (United States and Australia). They administered a questionnaire to local government managers in over 800 local governments in these countries to assess more than 30 fiscal management strategies that their local governments might use to address financial problems. Although there was considerable overlap in the top five strategies listed by managers in the two broad types of intergovernmental systems, there were striking differences as well. Both groups listed the following three strategies among their top five strategies in terms of relative importance: (1) improve productivity by better management, (2) improve productivity with technology, and (3) increase taxes. However, the top two strategies for managers in the unitary systems were the imposition of across-the-board cuts on all departments and reduction of capital expenditures, while these were ranked eighth and sixth respectively by the managers in the federal systems. Both sets of managers ranked the imposition of controls to limit population growth at or near the bottom (Danziger, 1991).

In rank order of importance by federal system managers (rank by unitary system managers in parentheses after each strategy), the top 15 strategies (Danziger, 1991, p. 174) were:

1. Improve productivity by better management (5).
2. Improve productivity with technology (3).
3. Increase taxes (4).
4. Increase user fees and charges (8).
5. Reduce work force (by attrition) (11).
6. Reduce capital expenditure (2).
7. Obtain additional intergovernmental resources (13).
8. Impose across-the-board cuts on all departments (1).
9. Increase long-term borrowing (6).
10. Contract out services to private sector (8).
11. Eliminate programs (8).
12. Defer maintenance of capital stock (15).

13. Increase short-term borrowing (12).

14. Shift responsibilities to other governments (10).

15. Impose controls to limit population growth (14).

A dictionary definition of a strategy is an adaptation that serves an important function in achieving evolutionary success. Local governments need strategies to help them evolve into more fiscally healthy entities. These strategies are conscious policies local governments pursue to help them adapt to their surroundings, which include changing conditions. Recall from Chapter 1 the discussion and diagram (Figure 1.1) of the fiscal manager's situation in which the arena the manager controls is relatively small.

We now turn to a discussion of strategies local governments can pursue in the present to help them survive and thrive in the future. These strategies are intended to help local governments not only to manage their resources more effectively, but also to expand and enhance their influence and control over their environments. These are actions that may be taken proactively at any time even though they are also useful to consider in reaction to stress.

In this chapter we outline an eight-point strategy for local governmental fiscal health. The number of strategies is somewhat arbitrary. As we have noted, some researchers have delineated dozens of strategies, while others cite only a handful of broad types of strategies. Neither of these approaches is wrong, since shorter lists collapse a lot of options under a smaller number of headings, while the longer lists are more useful when one is interested in exploring specific possible strategic behaviors in more detail. Our intent is to present a list that is long enough that we can make meaningful distinctions between and among strategies while not striving to compile an exhaustive list. In part, we are leaving room for readers to think creatively about new and different approaches that might be pursued under particular types of strategies.

This comprehensive approach is offered as a positive alternative to not having a plan for achieving fiscal health or to reliance on a single strategy, such as cutting costs, to address a local government's financial condition. It is also presented as a systematic approach for local governments to consider a wide range of ways to work on their fiscal health. In other words, it is designed as a set of deliberate or intentional actions local governments should contemplate to get themselves and keep themselves fiscally fit.

To borrow an analogy from personal health, we liken our eight-point strategy to an inclusive list of things people should consider to maintain and improve their health and well-being. We would not just commit ourselves to eating better food or getting more exercise. We would also consider changing our immediate environment by, for example, sitting in the nonsmoking section of a restaurant or installing air filters in our homes. We would also avoid risky behaviors such as smoking and abusing drugs while we also consciously engaged in behaviors known to promote safety such as wearing seat belts and bike helmets and getting regular physical examinations. So, while there is no guarantee that we are going to end up in tip-top physical shape and perfect health, we can enhance the likelihood that we will live longer, healthier lives if we pursue a multifaceted approach to wellness.

The same is true for local governments. A diversified strategy for attaining local fiscal health is preferable to reliance on one approach. Just as any prescription for personal health must be tempered with factual knowledge about the individual (e.g., medical history, age, ethnicity, lifestyle, and gender) and external factors (e.g., air quality, exposure to hazards) affecting the person, so too must decision makers exercise good judgment, consider community values, and weigh the risks and benefits of fiscal health strategies. Again, our medical metaphor can help us understand the point. If people ate too little food, they would risk anorexia or starvation. If they ate too much food, they would become obese and suffer from diabetes, heart disease, and other illnesses associated with being overweight. Getting proper exercise on a regular basis is a good thing, but too much exercise is bad for a person, just as exercising at the wrong time (e.g., if one is recovering from an injury) can be detrimental to one's health and well-being. Also, a person might have a set of values that affect particular actions they can pursue within a strategy. Just because an individual is a vegetarian does not mean that he or she does not need to get protein from some source.

As for local governments, community preferences must also be taken into account in charting a course of action for their financial future. For example, some communities have a strong aversion to debt-financed capital projects based on local values. There are always risks involved with any action undertaken to produce a desired effect or to avoid an unwelcome consequence. But, taken together, the following list of strategies is a good menu of options or checklist for making a plan to promote better fiscal health. It is a wide-ranging set of points for discussion. It is not suggested as a recipe to be followed with precise measurements and according to a set of required procedures. Rather, we are suggesting a set of ingredients that might go into the mix of strategies a local government pursues for fiscal health. Some communities will choose zestier, bolder strategies for their plans, and other communities will concoct more bland, predictable approaches that fit their situation and values, are more to their taste, and are in keeping with what is feasible in the local context at the moment.

This chapter outlines generic strategies, which means that there is a whole host of specific actions that might be undertaken to pursue any given approach. The choice of specific action is left to local decision makers. Some tactics might be considered politically unacceptable because they violate local tastes, preferences, norms, and values. For example, some leaders may have a bias against bringing in state and federal dollars because of the conditions or strings attached to those funds even if the infusion of outside dollars might make the local government more fiscally sound. Or some officials may object to policies they view as discriminatory against people with low to moderate incomes even though those policies might make the community more financially viable. Officials differ in their opinions on governmental borrowing, the appropriate level of cash reserves, and other decisions that have a direct effect on local fiscal health. And, even if they support debt financing for capital projects, a particular local government might be preempted from borrowing at a particular time because overlapping jurisdictions have already borrowed heavily so the same taxpayers are already being taxed to pay off other government debt. For example, a city's bond rating (which will affect interest expenses) is influenced by, among other factors, the level of debt on overlapping jurisdictions such as school districts and counties. In short, the strategies presented in this chapter are intended to stimulate a comprehensive approach to thinking creatively about approaches to achieving fiscally healthy local governments.

A further qualification is that these strategies are not mutually exclusive. Communities can pursue these strategies simultaneously. Readers must understand that trade-offs are inherent in policy decisions. Sometimes the pursuit of policies will cancel each other out. For example, one way of bringing in revenues is through economic development. However, if the community gives away too many incentives to lure in businesses, it will drain local government revenues. Likewise, if new businesses require a high level of local services, then the costs associated with service delivery may be greater than the additional revenues generated by the development. Depending on how much revenue officials anticipate from having higher valued properties and more taxable sales because people have jobs, this might be a prudent decision after all.

Officials also must think about both the short-term expected gain and the long-term effects of their policies. For instance, slapping on a new tax might be very lucrative to a local government at first, but over time, as individuals and businesses find ways to avoid the tax (say, by relocating to another jurisdiction where they can escape the tax), it may cost the government more than it gained in the short run.

This last point underscores the importance in any policy decision of considering both the intended impacts of policies and the unintended consequences of those policies. If it ends up costing a government more to collect a tax than it receives in revenues, then efforts to increase tax collections—while seemingly sensible—are not worth pursuing. For example, a city might consider levying a fee on users of the local park as a way of financing maintenance and equipment costs for the facility. However, people could choose to go to nearby parks that do not charge a fee. Or the costs associated with collecting the new fee might be higher than the revenues collected. And officials will want to consider whether there will be negative impacts on the community caused by fewer people using the park because they now have to pay to use it. These are just some of the issues local decision makers face in crafting the right strategy for their community.

The following eight strategies comprise a balanced approach to local fiscal health:

1. Be more efficient.
2. Expand the tax base.
3. Reduce the demand for services.
4. Shift costs to nonresidents.
5. Secure new sources of revenue.

6. Increase spending flexibility.

7. Improve management of existing resources.

8. Diversify revenue sources.

BE MORE EFFICIENT

Being more efficient means not wasting scarce resources. It means doing or producing more with existing resources or producing the current level of output with fewer resources. Making the most of resources entails such things as reducing overhead or costs that cannot be charged to particular functions the local government performs. It also means trying to achieve economies of scale.

Some steps local governments can take to try to be more efficient include eliminating duplication, introducing competition into the provision of services, sharing resources with other local governments or between departments, pooling of risk for workers' compensation to lower insurance rates, and recycling. For example, if two departments have different people answering their phones, it might be possible to have one person answer the phone for both departments, thereby saving the cost of one position.

As Chapter 8 on local boundary adjustments shows, one way local governments sometimes try to enhance their fiscal condition is through consolidation. Sometimes this entails the elimination of units of government. In other cases, efficiencies are sought by trying to consolidate departments, combining facilities, closing buildings, and the like.

Contrasted with the goods-producing sector, public sector output is often tied directly to the absolute level of staffing inputs. That is not to say that the public sector cannot institute some labor-saving innovations, thereby increasing efficiency. For instance, the city of Bowling Green, Ohio, has purchased new sanitation trucks that pick up garbage cans and set them back down with a mechanical arm. This has cut the need for labor and has lessened absenteeism and reduced claims for back injuries. As long as refuse is picked up properly and on time, citizens will be satisfied for the most part. But if the city were to cut back on police patrols, lifeguards, and emergency response personnel, the quality of service would decline noticeably and citizens would complain about the change in service. Even if citizens merely perceived that they were receiving less service due to labor-saving productivity improvements, it might not be feasible from a political standpoint to institute such changes.

For smaller communities, one approach might be to encourage more voluntarism on the part of skilled professionals in the community. By making the most of these scarce resources, the community is saving money and encouraging high-quality administration and services.

So one part of an overall fiscal health strategy is to look at a jurisdiction's operations for areas in which efficiency improvements could be made. By not wasting resources, a community can get more for their money and also alleviate the need to raise taxes.

Expand the Tax Base

Tax yield is the product of the tax rate times the tax base. One way to grow tax yield is to expand the base for local taxes. This is one of the arguments used for local governments engaging in economic development and land redevelopment (Pagano, 2003). By creating jobs, increasing the property tax base, and expanding sales by local businesses, communities can reap higher tax yields. For example, if a parcel of property is not generating property tax revenues because it has an abandoned warehouse on it, then it might make sense for the community to develop the property so that it will be on the tax rolls. Of course, there are substantial costs involved in this type of activity, including clearing the land, locating investors, and extending facilities and services to the site. However, the community may save other expenses such as extra policing if the vacant building was currently being used by drug lords for criminal activities. Getting the property back into productive use not only increases revenues, but also it might decrease other expenditures in the long run while making the area more attractive at the same time.

However, "it is very important to note the distinction between the fiscal health of a city and the economic health of the local economy. Although they are related, they are different concepts. It is not uncommon, even for local government officials, to lose sight of this distinction and to assume that whatever is good for the economy is good for the city's fiscal health" (Przybylski, Littlepage, and Rosentraub, 1996, p. 21). Readers are advised to note that the cost of the service to be provided to sustain economic development may be much higher than the revenue generated by the development (Ryan and Taff, 1996). Thus, we are suggesting that economic development policies are not necessarily the right way to go for every community seeking to shore up its fiscal health. For example, a community might generate revenues from slot machines or other gambling activities, but the unintended costs to the community might outweigh the benefits.

In fact, depending on how the community pursues economic development, it can actually jeopardize some aspects of fiscal health. For example, Swift County, Minnesota, lent a very large sum of money to a company to keep the business in the community. The company was paying back the loan and the company was providing jobs and income, which was helping finance the local government services besides providing other benefits to the community. Nevertheless, there was some risk involved in making a loan of this type. More directly to the subject of fiscal health, however, by making the loan the government had temporarily lost the opportunity to use those funds for other purposes. In other words, its cash balance fell because the money was no longer available to the county. This illustrates well the kinds of healthy debates that local government officials should have about policy. On the one hand, proponents of the loan can argue that it is a good investment and a prudent strategy for generating jobs and government revenues. On the other hand, it is also quite appropriate to question such an action from the standpoint of the balance sheet of the local government as long as the loaned funds are not available to the government.

Another way local governments attempt to increase their tax base is through strategic investments of their resources. For example, a community could advertise and promote local cultural events and arts festivals, subsidize home mortgages to try to attract a younger population, or redevelop an area such as a waterfront or downtown. By investing in these types of projects, the community hopes to recoup their expenditures in later years by generating revenues that would not have been available without public spending. There are, of course, risks involved in decisions like this. Sometimes investing in, say, a sports arena, pays off in terms of increased economic activity and public revenues. In other cases, these projects become a drain on the local treasury and, in retrospect, were a mistake. Carefully considering the economics of such investments is essential, and the timing of these investments is crucial. In the middle of a financial crisis would not be the time to undertake such investments, but they might be part of an overall strategy for steering out of a projected slow deterioration of fiscal health.

REDUCE THE DEMAND FOR SERVICES

If local governments can reduce the demand for services, then they might be able to avoid some expenditures. Some ways of cutting the demand for services do not necessarily result in lower quality services or less satisfaction by constituents. For example, a local government might focus on preventative measures to lessen the need for police and fire calls by residents. If the fire department succeeded in getting a majority of residents to install smoke detectors and buy fire extinguishers and taught people how to use them, they might reduce the number of costly trips by firefighters to put out fires that might be handled by property owners rather than be extinguished by professionals. Instituting such a program would be expensive, but it might pay dividends in terms of reduced costs to the local government and enhanced community relations.

Another more controversial way that local governments reduce the demand for services (consciously or not) is by making it difficult for people who would have higher demands for services to move into the jurisdiction or making it difficult for them to remain in the jurisdiction. Exclusionary zoning, minimum lot size requirements, refusal to accept low- to moderate-priced housing, and stringent building codes all favor people in upper-income brackets and discourage low-income people from residing in a community. Affluent people also have a high demand for services, but they also can afford home security systems and live in less crime-ridden neighborhoods. Conversely, low-income families living in small quarters may send their children to the local school system but contribute relatively little to the education budget. Or, in a city, they might be the biggest users of public facilities and human services that they do not pay for through local taxes.

These are just some of the ways that local governments reduce the demand for their services. While some of them are controversial on ethical grounds, they address the relationship between the need for services and the costs of paying for them.

SHIFT COSTS TO NONRESIDENTS

One way for local governments to make ends meet is to shift the cost of local government to nonresidents. By "exporting" at least part of the costs of local services, communities free up local resources. This strategy is also popular with the voters, so it is an appealing strategy to local politicians. Whether a local government can undertake this strategy often depends on whether the community has amenities or natural resources that outsiders want and are willing to pay for the privilege of using.

For example, tourist-based economies are able to charge non-residents for extra policing and fire protection, water supply and distribution, sanitation, and so forth. Since a very small community would have a hard time maintaining a police department at all, getting others to pay for one may be viewed as a benefit. However, sometimes the costs associated with throngs of visitors outweigh this perceived advantage. In addition, policy makers should consider the stability of revenues from tourism. If a competing destination suddenly becomes popular, the local government may see its tourism-derived revenues plummet. How vulnerable to the vagaries of the tourism market does a local government want to be?

Some of the mechanisms local governments might consider for "exporting" taxes include charging fees for nonresidents to use community facilities such as pools and parks, instituting a local-option sales tax if a lot of retail sales are to nonresidents, charging fees for parking lots that tend to be used by nonresidents, and taxing tickets for transportation to and from an island community. There are lots of ways that local governments can pursue the strategy of shifting the cost of local government to outsiders, and it should be considered an option within an overall strategy.

SECURE NEW SOURCES OF REVENUE

One strategy to make local governments more fiscally viable is the acquisition of new revenue sources. Sometimes this means looking inside the community for untapped sources of revenue, such as charging fees for services that were heretofore provided free of charge. Charging greens fees for the municipal golf course, charging an entrance fee for the community pool, or charging for pet licenses are possible sources of revenue that are currently being overlooked.

Frequently this strategy means that a community must look outside itself for new sources of revenue. State and federal grants-in-aid are the primary source of external funds. But local governments also sell services such as snow removal, trash collection, policing, and fire protection to neighboring jurisdictions. An important caveat about intergovernmental grants is that they come with strings attached. They usually require some level of local matching funds and they often are available for a finite period. Many local governments have gladly received federal dollars to add police officers to the local force. After the period of federal funding for the positions ended, local officials faced the prospects of either raising the funds to continue the position from local sources of revenue or making the politically unpopular decision to lay off the officers the community was accustomed to having on the beat.

So, while seeking new sources of revenue is an essential component of any effective strategy for ensuring local fiscal health, decision makers must exercise due caution. One unavoidable problem is that the time horizon of elected officials is usually shorter than the trajectory of their decisions. So a city council could approve the receipt of an external grant that saddles the community with obligations that come due after its current members leave office.

Increase Spending Flexibility

Another strategy to help smaller local governments gain fiscal health is to increase their spending flexibility. The ability to reduce their expenditures fairly quickly or to shift expenditures rather nimbly is advantageous to small local governments. Given their relatively small budgets, it behooves small governments to be able to effect changes quickly. For example, a local government may choose to contract for services rather than invest in the buildings, personnel, and equipment that lock a community into expenditures for a long time. Perhaps a small community can use mobile units (e.g., a bookmobile) to deliver services where they are needed at a particular time and then change or curtail the service more readily than if they built permanent infrastructure (e.g., branch libraries) that fix the location of the service.

This is, in part, a form of insurance. If a small community experiences even a relatively minor change in demographics, it can have a major impact on the demand for services. If the local government is locked into providing a fixed amount of service to an area, it incurs a financial burden.

IMPROVE MANAGEMENT OF EXISTING RESOURCES

This strategy seems self-evident, but to enhance the fiscal health of a local government it is important to consider better ways of managing resources. For example, a community might change policies to reduce risk, thereby saving money. By preventing job-related injuries, the city might be able to reduce some of its costs associated with absenteeism and workers' compensation. Another option is to manage the government's staff so as to avoid paying overtime to employees. Investing cash in order to receive a higher rate of interest is an obvious way to improve a local government's financial picture. In addition, if the economic environment and creditworthiness of the municipality will allow, a community should refinance municipal debt to more favorable terms. Doing a better job of tax collection will also help the government with its fiscal health.

In some cases, a community could manage its resources better by examining how it is currently doing things and identifying opportunities for better management practices. For example, a city could decrease the frequency or coverage of services provided (e.g., trash collection, maintenance of buildings and infrastructure, street cleaning, landscape maintenance, painting, and so forth). We are not advocating management changes that are "penny-wise and pound-foolish," causing the municipality to pay more money down the road for bringing back a decaying infrastructure that has not been maintained. However, if the city finds that it is spending as much on maintaining areas that do not deteriorate as readily as others, then this represents an opportunity for changing how upkeep is managed.

DIVERSIFY REVENUE SOURCES

A local government that is overly dependent on one source of revenue is vulnerable to influences that might affect that particular stream of income. So one component of a sound strategy for increasing local government fiscal health is consideration of alternative revenue sources. Again, this is something that must be tailored to local circumstances and opportunities. If a city happens to have a "cash cow" like a power plant, a ski resort, or other stable, well-heeled industry within its borders, then it is naturally easy for the jurisdiction to pass on the cost of local government to this major generator of government revenues. But most jurisdictions do not have the luxury of a single source of revenue that can pay for most of the cost of local government.

If a local government is very dependant on revenues from a particular footloose manufacturing plant, then the community might be more vulnerable than it would like to be. That one company can extract all kinds of concessions from the community because the community so desperately wants to retain the revenues from the company. Also, if government programs on which citizens have come to depend are wholly dependent on funds that a local legislator is able to garner from the state or federal government, what will happen to services if that lawmaker retires, decides not to run, or is defeated in an election? So, while it makes perfect sense for a community to take advantage of its assets and opportunities, it is important for officials to be mindful of the adage about putting all of one's eggs in one basket. If anything happens to the basket, then they are left holding nothing. So it is prudent to think about ways to diversify the sources of revenue on which the government depends.

SUMMARY AND CONCLUSION

The purpose of this chapter has been to discuss strategies for achieving and maintaining local government fiscal health. It is a complex topic. For one thing, there are myriad ways that local governments can engage in adaptive behaviors to make themselves more fiscally sound. Also, some practices are more reactive to fiscal stress and underscore the need for local government officials to try to think ahead about how the actions they undertake now will affect their jurisdictions' fiscal health in the future. There are no simple answers or right or wrong way to go, for the most part. Taking a contingency approach is the most prudent way to go. Studies have shown that the kinds of strategic responses local governments make when the source of fiscal stress is temporary (e.g., due to a recession) differ from their actions when the shortfall in revenues is more permanent (e.g., through a constitutional revenue-limitation measure). State laws, demographics, and many other variables affect the choice of options local governments should pursue.

This chapter has recommended a balanced, comprehensive approach to strategic planning about fiscal health. It is arguing for a more long-term plan than a quick fix such as just cutting spending or raising taxes. Interestingly, some research has found that fiscal stress is sometimes the stimulus needed to get local governments to undertake strategic planning for productivity improvement. In deciding among options, local governments must consider local tastes, values, norms, and preferences. Communities have different opportunities and approaches that local constituents and leaders will deem acceptable. It is also essential to consider unintended consequences and long-term effects of policies and not just the immediate impact of particular strategies.

DISCUSSION QUESTIONS

1. "Mock" County had traditionally had a very large cash balance. Over the past few years a number of factors (e.g., loss of a major industry, escalating costs of employee benefits, unexpected expenditures, decline in state and federal aid) had depleted this reserve of cash as expenditures were consistently outstripping revenues. An analysis of the county's finances revealed that the county was heading for financial problems if it did not take action soon to keep revenues more in line with expenditures. The chair of the county's finance committee, a county commissioner, stated, "It is obvious that there is only one thing we can do to solve this problem. We simply have to raise taxes." Another member of the committee suggested that the county explore alternative policy options for dealing with the county's financial situation, which everyone agrees must be addressed. Your job is to outline a number of options for the commissioners to consider. Draft a memo to the finance committee describing options for the members to consider.

2. How do you see values and ethics entering into the choice of options for achieving fiscal health objectives? In other words, consider dilemmas or value conflicts that might arise in the pursuit of various strategies. For example, are there trade-offs between fairness and equity, on the one hand, and efficiency, on the other hand, that might be

controversial in discussions about how to improve a city's financial condition?

REFERENCES

Beekman, P. (2003). Executive Summary, *Paths to Performance in State & Local Government.* Syracuse: Maxwell School of Citizenship and Public Affairs.

Berry, F. S. (1994). Innovation in public management: The adoption of strategic planning. *Public Administration Review, 54,* 322–330.

Danziger, J. N. (1991). Intergovernmental structure and fiscal management strategies: A crossnational analysis. *Governance: An International Journal of Policy and Administration 4* (2), 168–183.

MacManus, S. A. (1993). Budget battles: Strategies of local government officers during recession. *Journal of Urban Affairs, 15* (3), 293–307.

Pagano, M. (2003). City Fiscal Structures and Land Development. A discussion paper prepared for the Brookings Institution Center on Urban and Metropolitan Policy. Washington, DC: The Brookings Institution.

Przybylski, M., Littlepage, L., and Rosentraub, M. S. (1996). Philanthropy, nonprofits, and the fiscal health of cities. *Nonprofit and Voluntary Sector Quarterly 25* (1), 14–39.

Reschovsky, A. (1997). Are city fiscal crises on the horizon? Chapter 23 in D. Netzer, and M. P. Drennan, (eds.) *Readings in State and Local Public Finance* (439–464). Oxford, UK: Blackwell Publishers, Ltd.

Ryan, B., and Taff, S. J. (1996). *Estimating Fiscal Impacts of Residential Developments in Smaller Communities.* Minnesota Extension Service, University of Minnesota.

Shelton, M. W., and Albee, T. (2000). Financial performance monitoring and customer-oriented government: A case study. *Journal of Public Budgeting, Accounting & Financial Management, 12* (1), 87–105.

Stipak, B., and O'Toole, D. E. (1993). Fiscal stress and productivity improvement: Local government managers' perspective. *Public Productivity & Management Review 17* (2), 101–112.

TEN
Conclusion

The fiscal health of local governments is important from a variety of perspectives. To local officials, the fiscal health of their jurisdiction can be an asset or a liability in reelection campaigns. To citizens, fiscal health translates directly into taxes and services. It is important to them that they receive a certain level of local public services at costs they deem to be acceptable. To the business community, local government fiscal health is important because it affects the ability of local governments to provide essential services on which they depend at reasonable costs compared to comparable services available in other jurisdictions. To the states, local government fiscal health is important because it affects the states' bond rating and because the services they provide affect the quality of life and health, safety, and welfare of citizens statewide. The inability of local governments to finance services such as education, garbage collection, water, sewer, police, and fire is important from the states' perspective. If nothing else, states should be interested in how state policies help or hurt the fiscal health of local governments.

This book has focused on the fiscal health and condition of local governments. The focus has primarily been from the perspective of small to medium-sized local governments. However, states play a pivotal role in the financial well-being of their local governments. Among other things, states determine the powers, authority, and limitations local governments have for providing services and raising revenues; share financial resources with their local governments; and impose mandates that may have financial implications for local units of government.

Capacity-building activities are undertaken by a number of actors in the governance system to enhance the ability of local governments to deal with changes and fiscal stress. Among these, associations of municipal and county governments at the state level are of key importance. Most states have a league of cities or municipalities and an association of counties, which serve as lobby organizations on municipal and county matters. Some states have separate associations of public authorities or special districts. Some have multiple municipal associations, for example, that separately represent larger cities, boroughs, and townships. School districts have their own statewide associations. These organizations parallel similar organizations working at the national level to lobby national officials about state issues.

Importantly, all of the municipal and other associations also play key roles in generating and disseminating information to their local government members. This often includes training programs and extensive publications that can improve the managerial, technical, and financial capacity of their member governments. Annual conferences are a key networking feature provided by these organizations. Similarly, many foundations operate programs to build local government capacity, such as training in visioning and strategic planning. Along with these capacity-builders are state governments themselves. State agencies, such as departments of community affairs, often administer local government training programs and develop and produce publications that can enhance the financial condition of their local governments. Many legislatures have local government commissions that produce research studies and help to explain state laws affecting local government.

Sometimes, despite the ongoing efforts of local governments to maintain fiscal health, they find themselves in a crisis situation. They may not be able to meet payroll, pay bills, make payments on bonds, or pay withheld taxes for employees. In such cases, special remedial measures will be undertaken to bring the locality's finances back to health.

States may play four potential roles[1] in dealing with local government fiscal crises (Fig 10.1). The state could *predict* local government fiscal crises. This might happen through routine monitoring of local government budgets, auditing local government finances, or an elaborate monitoring system using an array of techniques and measures. If a state did anticipate a local government entering a financial emergency, the state could step in to *avert* the crisis by taking steps to keep the local government back from the brink. This could take the form of informal consultation, putting the local government on notice that they are being watched carefully, or providing temporary financial assistance to help the local government through a difficult period in its finances. This might happen if the state were alerted that a major employer that constituted a large share of a local government's tax base was exiting the community; the state might, for example, help the local government make bond payments or pay its vendors while the local government figured out how to deal with its finances over the long haul. If a local government was already in crisis mode, the state could potentially help *mitigate* the impact of the problem through various means, including technical assistance, placing controls on local spending, offering some kind of bailout or stopgap financing, or placing the local government under the control of an oversight board. Once a local government has passed the crisis stage, the state might attempt to *prevent a recurrence* of the financial emergency. This might take the form of intensified monitoring of the local

---

[1] This section borrows from Honadle, B.W., The States' Role in U.S. Local Government Fiscal Crises: A Theoretical Model and Results of a National Survey, *International Journal of Public Administration*, 26 (13), 1431–1472.

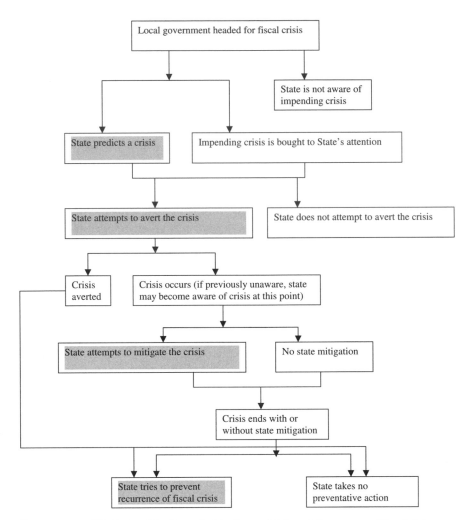

Figure 10.1   *The Role of the States in Dealing with Local Government Fiscal Crises*
Source: Honadle, B.W., "The States' Role in U.S. Local Government Fiscal Crises: A Theoretical Model and Results of a National Survey," *International Journal of Public Administration.*, Vol. 26 (13), 1431–1472.

government's finance or following up to make sure that the local government implemented reforms in its financial management practices.

Local government fiscal health is a broad term we have used to describe the condition of a local government's finances. As this book has shown, there are many terms in the lexicon on fiscal health that are closely related to this general concept. Fiscal stress and fiscal strain basically refer to how heavily a jurisdiction is taxing itself relative to its tax base. So a community might be experiencing increasing fiscal strain, meaning that its taxpayers are paying relatively high taxes, but the fiscal health of the jurisdiction is still in good shape.

A fiscal crisis, however, occurs when a local government is in an emergency situation. A local government on the verge of bankruptcy, unable to pay its creditors and vendors, in default, insolvent, unable to meet payroll, or behind in its withholdings for IRS is a local government in crisis. Clearly, these are the most serious cases of fiscal malady.

The purpose of this book has been to examine the concept of fiscal health, ways of monitoring local government fiscal health or condition, causes and consequences of local government fiscal health. As a part of this exercise, we have performed a review of macroeconomic trends and have examined strategies that may be undertaken to strengthen a local government's fiscal health or condition.

One of the key lessons of this book is that there are relatively few things that local government fiscal managers totally control. Local governments can influence some factors determining their fiscal health, such as the amount of state aid they receive, local economic development, and sometimes local government boundaries through such procedures as annexation and consolidation. Sometimes a local government can adapt to changing demographics, national economic trends, the prevalence of natural disasters and climate-related costs, and other drivers of local government fiscal situations. Beyond that, there are a great many influences over a local government's finances that, at least in the short run, a local government can only appreciate or take into account in its planning. But they can do nothing meaningful to mitigate or change these forces. Perhaps one of the best examples would be a recent change in the Governmental Accounting

Standards Board (GASB) rules for reporting as they pertain to local governments.

GASB sets generally accepted county principals. These are the rules for reporting financial information for state and local governments. GASB 34 (Mead, 2002; Statler, 2000) is a major revision of the current way of reporting. An in-depth treatment of this change is beyond the scope of this book's focus on fiscal health.[2] But it merits mentioning that these revised rules will provide important new information that has a bearing on how a local government's financial situation will be interpreted. For example, the new standards ask governments to think more like businesses. Infrastructure will be recorded as a capital asset and will be expensed through depreciation. Current accounting principles do not require reporting of infrastructure costs such as streetlights, roads, storm drains, bridges, tunnels, and so forth. That is because, as immovable objects, they are thought to be of value only to the government. But they are now going to be viewed as major community investments and, as such, will be accounted for accordingly.

In some cases the fiscal health of local governments will look better after implementation of GASB 34; in other cases it will look worse. It all depends on special circumstances of the local government. For example, by including long-term debt and other liabilities, it may reduce the local government's equity. Conversely, including infrastructure assets on the balance sheet might improve the equity of some local governments. Some observers of cities that have gone to the new model have found that GASB 34 makes local government finances just look different, not necessarily better or worse.

Although some critical factors such as the GASB 34 revision are beyond the control of local governments, it is still good for

[2] Refer to (http://www.westerncity.com/NOV00GASB.htm) for detailed information on GASB 34.

local governments to at least be cognizant of such factors. For one thing, being aware that there is a difference between factors over which local governments can exert meaningful control or influence and those that are more or less given facts of the situation helps sort out priorities for local decision makers. Also, local governments may, in the long run, take these factors into account by working around, say, a trend toward less state or federal aid. In other words, over time, local governments have more opportunity to adapt to changes from outside that cause them fiscal difficulties. In the short run, they may be forced to scramble for a quick fix to such obstacles.

Local governments bear substantial responsibility for their own fiscal wellness. They should do periodic checkups to gather information about their fiscal condition. The data gained through these examinations can be used for trend analyses (that is, self-comparisons over time or trends) or for comparisons with a reference group of other local governments. Depending on how sophisticated these monitoring tools are, these checkups can be very worthwhile in early detection of problems so they can be fixed or treated. By looking at indicators closely, local governments can diagnose the underlying causes of their fiscal health and address them before these problems become more systemic. For instance, if there is an early warning that a local government is starting to deplete its cash balance, the local government might decide to deal with that issue now rather than reach the point where its bond rating dips or the jurisdiction finds itself unable to pay its bills.

A good fiscal health monitoring program also has other advantages for local governments. One of these is the ability of local officials to be able to communicate about the local government's financial situation with taxpayers, voters, state legislators, or other stakeholders. For example, it might be easier to convince the voters to support a tax increase if officials can show a trend of decreasing intergovernmental aids. Or it might be easier to educate state legislators about the need for additional state aid if local officials can document a decline in a local government's tax base due to decline in an industry on which the locality has depended for much of its revenues. Resorting to user fees to make up for a declining revenue source might be more palatable to constituents if they had information on trends in local finances to explain why the local government officials have to do something to make up the gap between revenues and expenditures. And if popular services must be cut, having data on hand in an understandable format will make the politician's job somewhat easier by showing the need to trim costs in order to avoid higher taxes.

Such checkups are also excellent ways to orient newly elected officials about the finances over which they now have responsibility. Chapters 5 and 6 provide them with tools and indicators to perform these checkups. For them to become good stewards of local public resources, they must be knowledgeable about sources of funds, how money is being spent, and any potential problems that might need to be addressed.

Sometimes local governments undertake boundary adjustments in part to increase their tax base by, for example, increasing the amount of developable land within their jurisdiction. Such decisions are politically very sensitive both for the jurisdiction seeking expanded territory and for the local jurisdiction being faced with a smaller area. This book has presented a list of considerations or questions local governments should ask to help them understand the likely consequences of a boundary change on their local government's fiscal health. A local government may lose tax base through being on the losing end of annexation, but they may simultaneously decrease some expenditures. So, the question of whether local government boundary adjustments are good or bad for local finances is an empirical issue. The results may not be what one expects. For example, local government consolidations do not usually result in lower costs of government services even though they may lead to other benefits from the perspective of those favoring the consolidation.

Local governments must think strategically if they want to have good fiscal health. This means considering a range of actions designed to make local governments more efficient, expand their tax bases, reduce the demand for services, shift costs to nonresidents, secure new sources of revenue, increase spending flexibility, improve management of existing resources, and diversify revenue sources. Such a holistic or comprehensive approach to strengthening local fiscal health is more likely to yield better results than simply pursuing a single-minded course of action such as raising taxes or cutting spending.

In keeping with this holistic approach, in this book we have suggested periodic use of a variety of tools for analyzing fiscal health. Other tools are available, but we consider the tools we have presented in this volume to be especially well suited to small to medium-sized units of local government. These tools have the advantages of being simple, easy-to-understand, relatively inexpensive, and yet highly informative. Each tool has a particular strength (Honadle and Lloyd-Jones, 1998), but all work from a fundamental financial analysis of ratios and trends to examine what has occurred in recent history to provide a snapshot of where the local government is likely to be headed in the future.

To support some of the empirical signals generated by the tools, comparisons to other local governments can also provide a valuable benchmark against which to measure local government finance. Such relative quantitative analysis need always be strengthened by proper interpretation and feedback provided only though close interaction with local government officials. As demonstrated in Chapter 7, direct inference from analytical methods alone can often lead one to a false conclusion of strong or weak fiscal condition.

This book has provided a framework in which local government officials, scholars, students, and practitioners can thoughtfully plan, analyze, debate, and seek to ultimately improve the fiscal health of local governments. The study of local government finance and strategies for how best to manage local finances is as much an art as a science. We have attempted to impress upon the reader that no right or wrong answers or single method or procedure necessarily exists when working with local governments. Every situation is unique, and each situation is cast in its own context, which may validate or invalidate a successful approach or strategy employed elsewhere. Consequently, drawing on practical experience and using good judgment can often lead one to a more appropriate conclusion. Common sense, augmented by a fresh awareness of one's field of control, influence and appreciation will always serve local government officials well.

One of the main purposes of this book has been to increase the capacity of local governments to manage their finances. Figure 1.2 (A Fiscal Capacity Framework; Honadle, 1981) in Chapter 1 provided a conceptual framework for understanding the various tools, techniques, approaches, and strategies contained in the volume. This book has encouraged local governments to *anticipate* change so they can *influence* the future, rather than simply be buffeted around by their environments. This book is also helping them *devise policies* or effective strategies in response to perceived needs and influences. We are suggesting that a comprehensive program of fiscal health monitoring is essential for diagnosing and "treating" financial problems before they become serious. The book has also suggested a variety of alternative service delivery methods to help local governments *manage their resources* more efficiently and effectively. Finally, by periodically *evaluating* governmental activities, local managers have useful information about whether they are doing the right things, how well they are doing them, and whether they are doing them in an appropriate amount. The states can also assume an important role in ensuring the fiscal capacity of their local governments through conscious efforts to predict, avert, mitigate, and prevent future fiscal crises by local governments (Honadle, 2003). If this book has had an overriding theme or message, it is that prevention of fiscal problems is preferable to reacting to a crisis that could have been averted.

REFERENCES

Honadle, B. W. (1981). A capacity-building framework: A search for concept and purpose. *Public Administration Review, 14,* 575–580.

Honadle, B. W., and Lloyd-Jones, M. (1998). Analyzing rural local governments' financial condition: An exploratory application of three tools. *Public Budgeting & Finance, 18* (2), 69–86.

Honadle, B. W. (2003). The states role in U.S. local government fiscal crises: A theoretical model and results of a national survey. *International Journal of Public Administration, 26* (13), 1431–1472.

Mead, D. M. (2002). The role of GASB 34 in citizen-government accountability relationship. *State and Local Government Review, 34* (1), 51–63.

Statler, B. (2000). *Why is GASB 34 such a big deal?* Retrieved June, 2002, http://www.westerncity.com/NOV00GASB.htm.

About The Authors

Beth Walter Honadle is Director of the Center for Policy Analysis and Public Service and Professor of Political Science at Bowling Green State University in Bowling Green, Ohio. In this position she has developed the Fiscal Analysis Capacity Training (FACT) program for local governments based on the Fiscal Health Education Program she created at the University of Minnesota. These are educational programs for small to medium-sized local governments to help officials strengthen the financial condition of their jurisdictions. From 1990 to 1999 she was Professor of Applied Economics and Adjunct Professor of Public Affairs at the University of Minnesota, where she was also Program Leader for Community and Economic Development for the Minnesota Extension Service from 1990 to 1993. From 1985 to 1990, Honadle was National Program Leader for Economic Development in the Extension Service at the U.S. Department of Agriculture (USDA) in Washington, D.C. From 1979 to 1985, she was an economist and leader of the Organization and Delivery of Local Government Services project in the Economic Research Service, Economic Development Division, at USDA. During that period she was the first executive editor of *Rural Development Perspectives*. From 1986 to 1987 she taught Intergovernmental Relations as an adjunct professor in the public administration program at The American University in Washington, D.C. She has also done international consulting in Egypt and

Ukraine. Trained in the fields of public administration, economics, and political science, Honadle has published in such journals as *Public Administration Review, Economic Development Quarterly, Journal of the Community Development Society, Hamline Journal of Public Law and Policy, International Journal of Public Administration, Public Management, Public Productivity Review, Public Administration and Development, Publius, Public Budgeting & Finance, Economic Development Review, Government Finance Review, The Regionalist,* and *Journal of Regional Analysis & Policy.* Her Ph.D. in Public Administration is from the Maxwell School at Syracuse University. Honadle's current research focuses on the role of states in dealing with local government fiscal crises and on intergovernmental relations involving special district governments.

James M Costa is Vice President of Corporate and Investment banking at SunTrust Bank in Atlanta, Georgia. At SunTrust, Costs is responsible for the development and implementation of strategies to optimize the performance of SunTrust's large corporate and investment banking portfolios. Some of the primary areas in which he is presently involved include development of credit risk hedging programs, risk adjusted profitability analysis, economic and regulatory capital attribution, and macroeconomic forecasting and stress testing.

Costa has held a number of positions in commercial and investment banking and is a frequent speaker at international financial risk management conferences.

Prior to joining SunTrust, Costa was Associate Director of Portfolio Research at FleetBoston Financial in Boston, Massachusetts. There he was responsible for the development of a variety of financial models to manage risk for all Fleet commercial and corporate lines of business.

Before going to Fleet, Costa held the position of Research Associate and Adjunct Professor of Economics at the University of Minnesota. While at Minnesota, Costa's teaching and research interests focused on the areas of public finance, commodity futures and options trading, and the valuation of non-market goods via tradable permits. Before going to Minnesota, Costa managed sales and marketing for Merrill Lynch & Co.'s Private Client group.

Beverly A. Cigler, Professor of Public Policy and Administration at Penn State Harrisburg (PSH) received M.A. and Ph.D. degrees in political science from The Pennsylvania State University and has taught at five universities. She specializes in intergovernmental relations with key interests in alternative service delivery, public finance, government restructuring, state-local relations, counties, and government transformation. Her substantive policy fields are growth management and environmental policy. Cigler has received several national and state awards, including the PSH Research Award and a national public administration award for her intergovernmental research. Her Pennsylvania awards include Friend of County Government, Honor Roll of Distinguished Women, and Special Recognition from the Academy of Excellence in County Government. She also received a Distinguished Alumni Award from her alma mater, Thiel College. Bev was a Visiting Scholar in the Pennsylvania legislature from 2000–2002 and is currently a faculty associate in the Legislative Office for Research Liaison in the Pennsylvania legislature. She also directs a small research and outreach unit at PSH, The Pennsylvania Program to Improve State and Local Government. Bev has presented approximately 150 speeches, workshops and testimony to national, regional, and state associations of officials as well as government organizations. She has served on 10 editorial boards and held leadership positions in local and national associations. Much of her published work has received national and state funding and includes approximately 145 peer-reviewed articles and book chapters, with seven articles and essays in *Public Administration Review*. She has co-edited several books and written dozens of professional essays for practitioner audiences. Her latest research focuses on water and sewer infrastructure financing.

Index

Note: Boldface numbers indicate illustrations.